CONTES

THE NAME IT &

CLAIM IT GAME

WINeuvers for WISHcraft

Helene Hadsell

Updated by
Carolyn Wilman
THE CONTEST QUEEN

7290268 Canada Inc., dba Words For Winning
info@wordsforwinning.com

For details on quantity orders, contact the publisher at
orders@wordsforwinning.com

Hadsell, Helene
        Contesting: The Name It & Claim It Game
        WINeuvers for WISHcraft
Third Edition of The Name It and Claim It Game
1. Success. 2. Contests—Psychological aspects. 3. Rewards. (Prizes, etc.)
I. Hadsell, Helene. The Name It and Claim It Game. WINeuvers for WISHcraft

Paperback ISBN: 978-0-9939254-5-0
eBook ISBN: 978-0-9939254-6-7
Also available on Audible.

Cover design by Mark Lobo of doze!gfx.

DEDICATION

To Helene and all the great sweepstakes teachers that came before me. Not only did they make the hobby better, but they also changed countless lives.

Helene Hadsell
June 1, 1924—October 30, 2010

AFFIRMATION

Helene liked to repeat a simple phrase whenever she lectured, wrote, or counseled people:

"Let me be a channel to help people help themselves."

As she isn't here to state this phrase, may each of us reading these words affirm her prayer.

More Books

To read articles and stories from Helene Hadsell's archives, along with other adventures, audio programs, and videos, all for FREE, visit www.WordsForWinning.com

Also, get your FREE 15-minute SPEC-inspired Manifestation Meditation by signing up for the Words of Wisdom newsletter.

Books by Helene Hadsell

The Name It & Claim It Game

In Contact With Other Realms

Confessions of an 83-Year-Old Sage

A Man Called Friday

https://bit.ly/HeleneHadsellBooks

Books by Carolyn Wilman

You Can't Win If You Don't Enter

How To Win Cash, Cars, Trips & More!

https://bit.ly/LearnToWinSweepstakes

Online Workshops

WINeuvers for WISHcraft 2.0

Sweepstakes for Beginners

How to Win Giveaways on Social Media

RoboForm 101

http://bit.ly/CQWorkshops

TABLE OF CONTENTS

FOREWORD

I am not sure when I first heard about Helene Hadsell, but if you spend any time as part of the contest community, eventually, you do. How could you not? Helene was famous for winning every contest she entered and prize she desired, including a fully furnished home.

Sometime in the early 2000s, I was given a used copy of *The Name It & Claim It Game*. I felt very lucky as it had not been in print since 1988. I devoured it.

It wasn't my first introduction to positive thinking, visualization, mental projection, goal setting, etc. When I turned eighteen, my dad gave me my first motivational book, telling me, "If I can teach you at eighteen what I learned at thirty-six, you'll be way ahead of me."

After years of self-study, I concluded that my purpose was to teach others two things. First, how to bring more fun and excitement into their everyday lives by winning sweepstakes, and second, how to utilize a wide range of metaphysical methodologies as well as teachers—like Helene—to achieve that magical life.

I started my teaching path in 2004 by writing a book: *You Can't Win If You Don't Enter*, and also by publishing a newsletter. Then in 2008, I added a blog and a podcast to my platform. Every other Monday for several years, I chatted with the movers and shakers in the promotional industry, eager to share my message.

As I was always seeking dynamic guests for my podcast, I reached out to Helene, and she agreed to be on my show. I was beyond excited. (The audio interviews were recorded and can be found on my WordsForWinning YouTube channel, along with an entire video playlist here: https://bit.ly/HeleneHadsell.)

After our first interview, I was pretty brazen and bluntly asked Helene if I could come to Texas to meet her in person. She said no. A few days later, I received a phone call from her inviting me to visit. Helene said my spirit guides were so loud that she had to concede. (I'm loud in life, so it didn't surprise me that my spirit guides are also loud.)

That November, I found myself in Alvarado, Texas, in the presence of this amazing woman. To me, women like Helene were the original teachers of spirituality. Helene had mastered not only the Law of Attraction but also the art of manifesting, along with a whole slew of other extraordinary metaphysical skills. It's that very mastery that she imparts in all of her books. Helene also felt 'if she could do it, you could do it.' Although the hobby itself has changed tremendously over the past 50 years, the mind-mastery skills and the life lessons Helene imparts are timeless.

During my visit, Helene suggested that I pick up her gauntlet and start sharing with others what she had been teaching for decades. She didn't see herself teaching in person again and didn't want her messages to pass with her. I didn't do anything with her suggestion until now.

Because I interviewed her, wrote about her, and shared her teachings over the years, I received many requests for Helene's books, courses, and Blueprint readings. Finally, it was time for me to stop holding the gauntlet she'd given me and start running with it.

I reached out to her family and purchased the rights to update and republish her books. I was beyond excited to be putting out into the world what this intelligent, vibrant, and gregarious woman asked me to do over a decade ago.

Her son Dike sent me paperback copies of all of her books along with a CD with a digital copy of this book. I was astonished to discover that the 1988 printing I had was not her latest edition. Helene had updated it in 2010—the year she passed away. Her desire to teach never waned.

It is important to me that I maintain the integrity of Helene's work, so I've made only minor adjustments in this edition. I reformatted her book for current publishing methods (Print On Demand, Kindle, Kobo, Google Books, and Apple Books), added notes where required, and included a Recommended Reading section at the end so you may continue to learn and grow.

I've also made it easy for you to distinguish Helene's words from mine. **All of Helene's are in Arial font.** All of my words are in Times Roman font.

Just like Helene, it is my hope you understand her teachings and not only become a prize winner but a big winner in the game of life.

Carolyn Wilman, aka The Contest Queen
Best-Selling Author of *How to Win Cash, Cars, Trips & More!*

My Adventures With Helene

As stated in the *Foreword*, I was fortunate to spend four magical days with Helene. I am frustrated that I do not have a photographic memory. My memories are sporadic, as I only remember bits and pieces. However, hindsight is 20/20, and I wish I had kept a journal or notes during my stay.

Here is what I do recall.

Friday, November 14th, 2008

I landed mid-afternoon and headed off to rent a car. Helene lived in Alvarado, Texas, which is approximately 30 minutes south of Fort Worth and an hour from the airport.

As I wasn't going to have cell service or Internet at Helene's (it has changed since then), I stopped at Starbucks to update my email and connect with home, as calling long distance was going to be prohibitive on my flip phone. (It was 2008, after all!)

When I arrived at her doorstep, it was past dinner time. Helene was so sweet. She kept a plate warm for me, good home cooking. We sat at the table and talked about my day while I ate.

Then I got the tour. It was an open-concept home, and in the center was her conference area. This is where she held her workshops. I could only imagine what it would have been like to attend an original WINeuvers for WISHcraft workshop.

When Helene hosted full weekend seminars, she had a guest house for the students. As it was just me, I stayed in the back guest room.

Saturday, November 15th, 2008

After breakfast, I headed to Starbucks to check in, write, and get a Cinnamon Dolce latte. I brought one back for Helene, extra hot and double-cupped so it would survive the drive. She LOVED it! She had

11

never had a drink from Starbucks or a latte, and I remember how giddy she was sipping her first hot, sweet, foamy drink.

Conference Area

On my way to Starbucks, I spotted a roadside stand selling fresh pecans. Of course, on the way back, I stopped and bought two bags to bring home with me. What a treat!

When I returned, Helene said she wanted to buy some supplies to create Blueprints. She was out of the photo albums with the sticky pages she used. Off we went on a shopping trip.

I should say adventure. One of Helene's favorite sayings was Helen Keller's quote, *"Life is a daring adventure or nothing."* Anytime spent with Helene, no matter how mundane on the surface, was an adventure!

Our first stop was Rosa's Café, as by then it was lunchtime. The first thing we spotted when we walked in was a big sign advertising a sweepstakes.

You had to record a 30-second video describing your experience at the café. As Helene didn't have any modern video recording skills, I recorded her entry and submitted it on her behalf. She messaged me a few months later, telling me she had won a secondary prize. She really did win every contest she entered, and I got to witness it firsthand. While looking for pictures for this book, I found her video submission. I posted it on my Contest Queen YouTube channel. If you want to see it, here's the link: http://bit.ly/HelenesContestEntry.

We ended up going to several Dollar Trees and Dollar Generals, as none of them seemed to have enough of the specific photo albums Helene needed to make her Blueprints. In the end, we found a dozen or so.

Once we got back, we sat and enjoyed afternoon tea. Helene still had her coffee station set up in her kitchen from her workshop days. Coffee maker, kettle, mugs, teas, sugar, etc., all set out for anyone to enjoy a cuppa anytime they wished. It was the first time I'd ever had Irish Breakfast tea. To this day, it is still one of my favorites.

Later that evening, we watched a Made for TV movie: *The Two Mr. Kissels*. For some reason, I still remember the whole movie. It may be because, as crazy as the story was, it was based on real-life events.

Helene and I talked during the commercials. I can still see her sitting in her big easy chair with a heating pad on each armrest to keep her warm. I sat on the couch, tucked under a crocheted throw. The following year she mailed me that throw. The note enclosed said I won first prize as the best guest in 2008. I still have the note and throw.

We talked about how she manifested all of her adventures, prizes, and dreams. Helene told me there was one thing she still wanted to do; be a guest on The David Letterman Show. It was one adventure that never manifested for her.

Sunday, November 16th, 2008

I planned my whole trip around this day. Since I was coming to Texas, I thought, "Why not be in town for The DFWinners Sweepstakes Club monthly meeting while visiting Helene?"

Not only did I invite myself to the meeting, but I also invited Helene! Thankfully, the club was thrilled to have me as a guest. They were ecstatic when they discovered Helene was coming with me.

Just as I had done every day on this trip, the first stop on our way to Irving was Starbucks.

While we drank lattes, I worked on my laptop. Helene sure loved the sweet and foamy concoctions Starbucks had to offer. I could only imagine how often she would have been frequenting the store had she discovered them sooner.

Helene didn't want me to take any pictures of her during the trip, but she did let me snap a partial one using my computer camera. (See Helene tucked into the bottom right-hand corner?!)

Sadly, the resolution was perfect for the web but not great for print. Even so, I thought the memory was worth sharing.

I might not remember every detail of the weekend, but thankfully, I had the sense to blog about our visit to The DFWinners Sweepstakes Club monthly meeting. Here is what I wrote:

The DFWinners

> Last Sunday, I was lucky enough to attend the monthly club meeting of the DFWinners with Helene in tow. (See if you can

spot her in any of the pictures.) It was held at the Spring Creek BBQ restaurant in Irving, Texas. I found their club to be so different from the one I belong to.

My club, The Winner's Circle, only has twelve members. We meet once per month at a local restaurant. We have lunch, chat about the hobby, and have a scratch lottery ticket trade.

NOTE: We now meet twice a month on Zoom. Join us for our Virtual Contest Club Meeting. https://bit.ly/ContestClubMeetings

This meeting had twenty-nine people in attendance. I'm not sure how many members they have. They have a formal meeting format. Before the meeting starts, people line up to participate in the draws: stamped postcards, decorated envelopes, scratch tickets, 50/50, and Better Than Nothing. The meeting began with a Roll Call. Each person introduced themselves and what they had won since the last meeting—lots of cheering for each other. Even if someone's wins were low the past month, there were many words of encouragement.

They even have a wins board to track how many big wins they have had as a club.

Then I got up and spoke a bit about the hobby and answered questions about how the hobby is different between Canada and the United States. The shortlist of the differences are the lingo (contestor vs. sweeper), the taxes (in Canada, we do not pay income tax on winnings of any kind), there are virtually no mail-in contests left in Canada, and the number of local sweepstakes where participation is required is far greater.

I discovered later that the part of the meeting I spoke about was their Educational Session, where they learned something new to increase their odds of winning. The previous month they had made shaving cream envelopes.

Then they had their draws. I won the 50/50. WOOHOO! (I bought my daughter pink cowgirl boots with my winnings.)

After all the winning was done, they discussed club business. (The business section was very similar to the business section of my Toastmasters club meetings.) Since it was November, they talked about the Christmas party/meeting and the new executive for the following year. I then realized the four women sitting at the front were the President, Webmaster, Secretary, and Treasurer.

At the very end, Helene stood up and offered to host a few members as guests in her home one Sunday in the new year and teach them firsthand about attracting the wins they really want. They will have a draw for the five winners in January. Everyone was very excited at the prospect of being lucky enough to win an afternoon with Helene!

The two hours went by so fast. Helene and I had so much fun!!

Helene had told me she stopped entering sweepstakes years ago because she won everything she ever wanted. My winning energy was so contagious that by the time I left, we were in the process of winning her a new computer. (I seem to have that effect on people!) So we agreed once she won, my family would all come down for a visit, and we would get her all set up. I plan to ensure our trip coincides with another DFWinners meeting!

If you are traveling, see which sweepstakes clubs are in the area and attend a meeting if possible. It's a great way to be around fellow sweepers in between conventions.

On our way back to Helene's, I spotted a sign for frozen custard. I asked Helene what it was. She said it was similar to ice cream. We were like two little kids as we skipped dinner and ate custard instead. I remember sitting in the car, cups of custard in hand, giggling as we devoured our sweet treat.

Monday, November 17th, 2008

It was time for me to head home. After breakfast, I headed to the airport, but no trip to Texas would be complete without buying a pair of cowboy boots. I stopped at Cavanaugh's Boot City. I bought myself a pair of Justin Boots and my daughter a pair of pink cowgirl boots, which are currently tucked away in her keepsake box.

Sadly, I never saw Helene again. She passed away two years later. I will always be grateful for our time together, the lessons I learned, and the opportunity to share her wit and wisdom with you now.

PART ONE

INTRODUCTION #1

AN EXCITING CHALLENGE FOR YOU, THE READER:

Learn how you can play the game of life using positive thinking to win.

You may find this a bold and egotistical book. I hope you do. You may also find ideas that can guide you in the transformation of your life. If you feel like you've never won anything in your life, you CAN change that pattern and become a WINNER; that is, if you want to change.

Why was this book written? It was written for people who are unhappy and dissatisfied with their present status. Most of all, it was written for those of you who are willing to challenge your present ideas about life and change them when necessary.

What is the key to success—the key that opens the Magic Box where all goodies of life are stored? It resides in the mind: the vast computer that has the secrets of the Universe and of life itself. So much awaits us when we become aware of the mind and when we take control of it.

We can finally learn why things happen to us, which places us in control of our fortunes. No person and no circumstance can disturb our inner peace. Fear and tension vanish when you use positive control. Heartache and headache are exposed and dissolved. Everything becomes right when we learn to love in this new way. You possess all the capabilities for self-enrichment. You need only exercise these powers. As you begin, have no concern whether you are proceeding correctly.

Just begin.

Helene Hadsell

THE NAME IT
& CLAIM IT GAME

You'll see it when you believe it.
Helene Hadsell

The truly successful person is a positive thinking one. The more you cultivate and control a positive attitude, the more successful you become. As you develop positive thinking, success replaces failure until you can no longer fail.

No matter your past or present, you can change your future. Everyone has a different idea of what success is. To some, being successful in romance and love is the ultimate goal; some seek health and body-building programs; others want fame and fortune; and some need huge homes, cars, and money as a determining factor.

Unfortunately, some don't know what they want. They scatter their desires into so many avenues that they never really accumulate enough energy to make anything manifest for them. They run hot and cold, up and down, in and out of projects, never really stopping long enough to analyze why they are not successful. They never fully accept the idea that, with a positive attitude and control, they can materialize anything they need or want on the physical plane.

The following personal experiences that I'll share with you are not to tell you how great I am… but to clue you in on how great you are. There's a saying that tells you so: *"All these things that I do, you can do, and more."*

A number of years ago, my idea of success was to be able to enter contests and win, win, win—anything and everything that one could possess in this material world. I developed a desire, a goal, and a determination. I had read a book on positive thinking, and it left an indelible impression. I was out to prove to myself that anything the mind can conceive and believe, it can achieve with positive thinking.

STEP NUMBER 1: Set a goal.

If you *know* what you *want*, you can *have* it. I must make one thing clear regarding my entering contests since there are sometimes misconceptions as to why and how one wins.

I had no background, such as a writing talent, nor had I taken any writing courses at that time. I did not know anyone who worked for judging firms. In other words, I had no 'pull.'

My first experiment began when my husband expressed a desire to own an outboard motor since he enjoyed fishing. He called my attention to a contest sponsored by a soft drink firm: the prizes were outboard motors. The requirement was to complete, in twenty-five words or less, stating why you like to take 'Coke' on your outings.

My one entry was this: "I take Cokes on outings because I'm a lone-wolf fisherman, and Coke is my silent partner, contributing no yakity-yak, only refreshing enjoyment when called upon."

I came upon this idea when I imagined my husband, so I naturally wrote from his viewpoint. He certainly did like to go fishing by his lonesome, that is, until our two boys were old enough to enjoy fishing trips with him.

Three weeks after the contest closed, the phone rang, and a company representative informed us that we had indeed won an outboard motor!

I confess that prior to the announcement stating that I had won, every time the thought crossed my mind about the contest or the motor, I 'convinced' myself again and again that I would win. I was so determined to be positive I even asked myself, *"I wonder when they will let us know we have won?"* I had no negative doubts, such as *"I'll bet the contest is rigged."* (I'd heard that one quite often.) Nor did I entertain the thought that I wasn't lucky or that only clever people win. (Now, how does one acquire cleverness? Why one works at it.) So, you see, I refused to entertain any negative doubts.

STEP NUMBER 2: Never entertain doubts.

This nullifies all good, strong, powerful, positive currents.

The second contest I entered was a jingle-type, where one had to complete the last line of a phrase. The prize was a second telephone installed in your home with the bills paid for a year. I thought about how convenient it would be if I could have a phone installed in the kitchen since I spent most of my time in that part of the house.

When I sent off my three entries, I used the same positive thinking I had applied to my 'motor win.' I knew I would be a winner, and again I questioned how long it would take the company to inform me.

It took five weeks after the contest closed before I received the letter telling me I was a winner. I had no way of knowing which entry actually won.

In the meantime, we decided to move into a larger home and moved from Grand Prairie to Irving, Texas. The company that sponsored the telephone contest was kind enough to send a check instead of the phone service for a year.

By now, the family was quite impressed with their mother, who had only made two attempts at entering contests, and won both. In the next effort to win contests, the family joined in.

A request came from our daughter, then twelve years old: she wanted a bicycle. She called my attention to a contest advertisement in the Sunday paper's Comic Section. The requirement was to name a pony. We got so carried away this time that we submitted seven entries. She won a girl's blue bicycle four weeks after the contest closed. We had no way of determining which one of the names actually impressed the judges, but we did have great fun being creative and coining original, apt names. The following are the names that we sent: Foot-Prince, Him BUCK-too, Fancy Prance, Stirrup Dust, Stan Pedro, Twinkle Toes, and Prance Charmin'.

Our eight-year-old son, Chris, was next to put in his bid. He, too, wanted a shiny new bicycle. At that time, a candy contest was in progress, and the top prizes were bicycles. We were to complete, in fifteen words, why we liked their candy product. Again, we made a family project of writing ideas, and in this endeavor, we submitted four entries. Now the children were so sure we just had to win that we all waited eagerly for the mailman to bring us the letter making it official. We now realized, it took from two to six weeks after the contest closed before winners would be notified. And, of course, he won the bicycle.

This time we were interested in which entry actually won. We came up with this method: we submitted the first entry in his full name, Chris Vince Hadsell; for the second entry, we used only Chris Hadsell; the third signature was Chris V. Hadsell, and the fourth was C. V. Hadsell. This way, we were able to determine the winning fifteen words. They were: *"So colorful, so neat, so nice and plump; they're chewable pick-ups for a midday slump."*

The letter telling him he won was addressed to the name we used to submit this entry. We were describing why we like candy-coated licorice pieces. Children's contests are great to encourage family help.

This idea of keying entries like this was not original with us, as later we learned quite a few contestants used this method to key their entries and to know which one of their 'brain-children' actually won the prize.

At this time, there were so many contests and so many prizes; one had a choice of what one wanted, which to enter. Perhaps, instead, we had only become more aware of opportunities for obtaining the things we would like to have in life.

I inject this for anyone who sees this as luck. The fact that we did win the first time we entered helped us gain confidence. There is an old cliché that goes like this: *"If at first, you don't succeed, try, try again."* Had I not won on my first try, I feel my positive attitude would have urged me to continue to enter anyway.

I have since realized that with a positive-thinking outlook, there is no failure, only a delay in results. (Think about it.) The **imaging faculty** played a leading part in the goals I wished to achieve. I recommend, in order to play any game successfully, train your faculty of imagination.

If the prize appealed to us, we worked on that contest to win. Suffice it to say; we won bats, balls, radios, dolls, games, electrical appliances, and cash prizes. In other words, you name it, and we claimed it. I was reluctant at that time to vie for any contests that offered trips because I was afraid to fly. I had already told myself that if I did win a trip, I would not take it. So I never gave that type of contest any consideration or energy. In other words, I was content with the comforts like blankets, bicycles, and basics. But that soon changed.

The day our two sons, Dike and Chris, saw a contest for a trip to a dude ranch in Arizona, they said, "WOW, that might be family fun." I wanted to go, but flying was out of the question; however, we did enter the contest.

To make a long story short, we won the trip. Again, this contest called for children to name a pony. We submitted the same names we used in the other pony-naming contest and noted that this time, the name Stan Pedro was the winner. When the forms came about flight schedules, I requested we be allowed to go by train. I refused to go by plane. I did not realize it was a prepackaged deal for the winners, and fly; you must. When I refused, we were disqualified. We did, however, receive a nice second-place prize of a movie camera. However, my sons were very disappointed.

NOTE: Helene was lucky. Usually, if you decline a prize, you do not win anything. It's up to the discretion of the sponsor if they choose to offer you an alternate prize.

When I had time to consider the immaturity of my groundless fear of air travel, I had to do some powerful, positive thinking to convince myself that planes are quite safe. I told myself I would enjoy flying, and in the future, I would enter contests and vie for trips because they would be fun. In other words, I was conning myself for the big lift.

I finally convinced myself, with all that positive thinking, that the only way to go is to fly. I called this *The Die As You Fly* program, knowing my fears would die when I actually experienced the venture. In the meantime, I was scared stiff. What a challenge. What conflict. Wow!

STEP NUMBER 3: You can con yourself into anything.

By repeating it over and over, again and again. Until one day, it is incorporated into your thinking.

That is the way it is. Sometimes it takes longer, but I have found it is a very effective, surefire method once you incorporate it into your conscious-thinking program.

A family dude ranch trip was offered again the following summer in a children's contest, and this time, I informed the family that it would be our summer vacation. This particular contest was sponsored by a ranch-style bean company. It merely required one to submit one's name on the back of a label. It was a sweepstakes-type contest. Of course, we won it, and of course, we flew. To say I did not have apprehension would be a big, fat lie. I recall that all during the trip, I was in an 'in-fright' trance, convincing myself how great it was. (Who was I to tell them that if God had wanted us to fly, God would have given us wings?)

The family had such a great time that I could not deprive them of any future fun trips that they were now anticipating. I also did further reprogramming and told myself that on the next trip, I'd open my eyes and eat the meal served.

The next year, we won first prize for a family trip to Disneyland: my younger son, Chris, 'the fly-hi-boy,' insisted we win trips. (He is an Aries, and for some reason, they are always in the air.) We bugged him to draw the ugliest bug he could conjure up for this big deal. Talk about excitement; that really was one of the many highlights in the

Hadsell family's fun-n-game times. The trip was so delightful; I could have kissed the judges and sponsors. (Imagine kissing perfect strangers?! I still have never met one.)

In all our experience of contest winning, the prizes were always more than we had hoped for. If we won an appliance, it was always the latest model. The representatives from the companies were most kind, and usually, we got things not included on the prize list. For example, our trip to Disneyland stipulated a trip for a family of four—there are five Hadsells—yet they included all of us, gave us extra passbooks for park activities, plus a generous spending allowance. It was beautiful.

LET BIG BROTHER WIN THIS ONE
HE IS MORE PATRIOTIC THAN I

After the five-day family holiday on the dude ranch and the Disneyland trip, the boys' appetites were whetted for more travel and trip wins.

The next opportunity that presented itself for a trip, and proved interesting to boot, was geared for high school students. Requirements were to complete a two-hundred-and-fifty word essay on 'My Responsibility to America.' Two winners from each state would win a trip to the nation's capital for three days of touring and listening to government officials. The contest was sponsored by Rexall Drug Stores: I had noticed the blanks in the store one day and brought one home.

That evening at the dinner table, I was explaining the contest to the boys and elaborating on what an advantage it would be to visit Washington, D.C. I asked which one might like to make this trip. They both thought it over momentarily, then Chris said, "Let big brother win this one. He is more patriotic than I."

"Okay, the deadline is eight days from now, so you better do some serious thinking and get it on paper," I suggested.

May I say that even after several years of contesting, I was still the one that stimulated the interest it took to get rolling on a new one. The family dynamic of offering encouragement, suggestions, and ideas, plus their positive thinking, made it a most gratifying, family fun-and-game activity.

Dike's entry was so sincere and warm that when I read it, I could find only one mistake. That was in spelling. In my estimation, it was a sure winner. Now, all that was required was for the judges to make it official.

That evening we had out-of-town friends for dinner. Usually, I let my husband, Pat, read over the gems of wisdom (our entries) before I licked the envelope and sent them on their merry way to impress the judges. That evening, I was in a *show and glow* mood, for I was quite proud of Dike's originality, sincerity, aptness of thought, and clarity of presentation (rules the entry would be judged on). I just had to share it with our guests. I asked if they would care to have a sneak preview of a winning entry that would win our son a trip to Washington, D.C. At first, they thought I was kidding, but after reading it, I could see they were impressed.

When one of the guests handed the copy back to me, he asked, "Say, this is terrific, but how can you be so sure that it will win the trip?"

Honestly, one can get a bit weary with all the 'Doubting Thomases' floating around. I hope, for your sake, there are not too many in your environment.

Had I been a gamblin' woman, I would have made a bet. Instead, I said, "Give Dike your address, and he can drop you a card while he is in Washington, D.C."

I'll never do that again because it appeared that I might know the judges or have some pull, and it aroused suspicion. So that's a NO-NO: **NO Braggin' before Baggin'**… Remember that!

Dike was notified that he had won the trip four weeks later. He brought home many interesting experiences that he shared with us. (This was his first trip without the family.) I sent a newspaper story of his trip to our guests—I just thought they should know.

"Anything he can do, I can do better." was now our younger son Chris' attitude. He had an opportunity to prove his creativity very shortly. A popcorn company was sponsoring a contest asking children under fourteen years of age to draw an original of a popcorn

man. The top prize was a free trip to the World's Fair for that child and one adult. Besides the all expenses paid plane fare and three days stay at a downtown hotel, the winner would also receive one hundred and fifty dollars for spending money—my, what an exciting opportunity. I'd get to go to the Fair with him! Things were *poppin'*, and plenty of 'corny' ideas were exploding (we kept discarding), but when the nitty-gritty time came to concentrate on one idea, we came up with a winner. It was one of the three top winners in the nation. So, that year we saw the World's Fair.

"Can you top this?" was then Chris' challenge to his brother upon his return from the World's Fair adventure.

"Give me time, little brother." was Dike's reply.

Then it appeared on the scene, a trip just geared for Dike. He was to graduate from high school in June, and a month before school closed, the contest appeared. Ninety youths would be given the opportunity to tour Europe for six weeks. They would hostel all over the continent to remote villages by train, plane, boat, and bicycle.

The Wrangler Jean Company was sponsoring this one. The requirement was to write a fifty-word statement as to why you felt you could be a 'Goodwill Ambassador' to Europe. He wrote his entry, then immediately got ready to travel by getting his passport and required shots. When I say we are positive, I also mean we are prepared.

NOTE: This tip is important because being prepared tells the Universe you are serious about receiving the abundance it has to offer and that you are ready to reach your goals and dreams now.

A day before graduation, he received the wire: he was on the winning team. The experience of the tour is still considered one of the special events of his life. He still corresponds with several youths he met on the excursion. Upon his return, as Dike was sharing his travelogue and showing us slides of the places he had visited, Chris announced, "Say, that sounds exciting; it's my turn to go to Europe next summer."

A Clearasil contest made it possible for his wish to be fulfilled. The next July, he was jetting to Europe on what he called "A trip where only the elite meet, greet and eat." It was first class all the way: he claimed he had never seen such plush places and had such exotic food.

This particular contest was a sweepstakes. The number of entries in this type of contest is fantastic: some have drawn as high as 300,000 entries. Only thirty youths, fifteen girls and fifteen boys, were selected. He also had his passport and required shots in readiness prior to the official notice of the win. If you've got a positive attitude, flaunt it, but only in the family environment.

As I stated earlier, all five Hadsells were in the act of winning contests by using a positive attitude.

Daughter Pam had her place in the sun, also. Her interest slanted toward recipes and art entries.

She won cash prizes by submitting recipes to numerous national, as well as local, contests. It was one of her entries that won, for the family, a complete home library consisting of the fifteen-volume set of Childcraft and the twenty-volume World Book Encyclopedia.

In an art contest, it was her talent that snagged a stereo/record unit for us. She supplied us with radios through her endeavors in creativity. Pam, at one stage of the fun-and-game contest pursuits, declared, after winning five pairs of roller skates, "I get the impression I'm spinning my wheels."

After submitting an entry and winning an elaborate electric train set for the boys, we offered encouragement by telling her she was really on the 'right track.'

ALL THINGS COME TO HIM WHO WAITS

Thoughts are things.
Helene Hadsell

One year, before the Christmas HoliDAZE, my husband asked what I wanted for Christmas. At that time, I needed an electric skillet. I was already enjoying a steam iron, thanks to Proctor Silex; a new toaster from generous Sunbeam; a new coffee pot presented to me from Corning Ware; and an electric blanket, compliments of General Electric. Oh yes, I also had an electric knife, can opener, mixer, and toothbrushes from other sponsors.

I told the dear boy not to buy a skillet, as I was positive I'd be winning one shortly. In that month, I'd entered a number of contests with priority on that particular win.

When Christmas morning's gift-opening time arrived, the big, square box under the tree contained an electric skillet. My husband had bought one for me.

Between January 1st and 20th, I heard from three different sponsors, all congratulating me on my winning their prize of an electric skillet! How wonderful. I was now able to give them as gifts.

One spring, I had the inclination to remodel my kitchen. I was giving all the cabinets a fresh coat of pale-yellow paint. One morning after the mail delivery, I was leafing through a magazine, enjoying my morning coffee, when I noticed on page thirty-two: the Westinghouse contest display. Amid all the appliances pictured, I could see the stately, Coppertone stove, a perfect addition and a 'must' for my kitchen redecorating project. Somehow, my eight-year-old white stove had served its purpose and now looked ancient. I knew I could contribute it to the church auction to help raise funds for their projects. I neatly and discreetly, and mentally found the perfect place for it.

Fifteen hundred prizes were offered in the Westinghouse contest. The first ten prizes were complete laundry units. The second ten prizes were refrigerator-freezer units. The ten third prizes were colored stoves; other prizes were portable TVs and small appliances.

I disregarded all the prizes but the stove. The rules said to write a twenty-five-word statement on why you liked Westinghouse products. I was so enthused that I submitted five entries that evening.

This time I had a long wait because I entered immediately. (Usually, a contest is advertised and promoted several months before the deadline. After the closing date, there is a period of two to six weeks before the winners are notified.) In the meantime, I sewed curtains for the kitchen windows and installed the new flooring I had won in a local drawing. Every time I looked at my stove, I visualized a new, streamlined, Coppertone stove in its place.

NOTE: As many contests have moved online, the average lead time from start to finish has shortened dramatically.

At this time, I was acquainted with a number of people whose hobby was contesting. We would share ideas, discuss contests, and where one might be able to find blanks. We even formed a club that met once a month so we could encourage one another.

NOTE: Hundreds of sweepstakes clubs exist across the United States and Canada. You can find links to some clubs on my Contest Queen website. http://bit.ly/SweepstakesClubs

One day, about five months after the contest closed, a friend called to inform me she had just been notified that she was a winner of a portable TV. Later, I heard from a number of Westinghouse winners in the area. I hadn't heard a thing.

I assumed my timing was off, but regardless of Westinghouse, I definitely would have the stove in my kitchen. I was so positive; I could almost touch it by now. That is how vivid and real it had become to me. I kept thinking of the phrase, 'thoughts are things.' I was convinced that if enough positive mental energy is sent out, things eventually manifest in the physical. Another phrase that is most comforting, and one that which should be incorporated into your thinking, is, **Anything the Mind Can Conceive—And Believe—It Can Achieve**. I was out to prove it to myself again and again.

In the middle of the week, I received a legal-sized envelope with a congratulatory letter and a check for $1,000. I was a second-prize winner in a spray paint contest that offered all prizes in money. Talk about being elated! Don't you see? Here was my 'stove,' with money to spare.

When I get excited, the first thing I do is call my husband so that he can share in my enthusiasm. My opening statement is usually, "You'll never believe this." His answer is usually, "Try me, kid; I haven't heard it all yet." I bought the Coppertone stove and had it installed the following day. I was so *pleased* with 'Project Stove.' You would have thought it had dropped from Mt. Olympus.

Ten days later, I received another letter. This one was from WESTINGHOUSE. It stated that in the process of awarding prizes, someone had overlooked notifying me of my third-place win, a stove!

I was stunned. If one is ever able to become unglued, this could have been the perfect time. The district manager called me several days later to ask when he could have the stove delivered.

I explained the recent stove purchase. "No, I didn't get the Westinghouse brand. I ran into a clearance sale of stoves at Sears and found one almost like the Westinghouse model, and I was able to save $85.00 below the usual cost."

The district manager was most kind and understanding. If I had purchased a Westinghouse stove, the full retail price would have been reimbursed. This is how I obtained a new washer-dryer unit in lieu of a stove. Now that wasn't too dramatic because I hadn't really given a washer/dryer unit any consideration.

One weekend, we went to the Texas State Fair in Dallas. I became intrigued with the color TVs and their sharp, colorful, clear, crisp pictures. That's when I got the idea that our next project would be to win a color TV. I gathered all the positive thinking I could conjure, turned on the imaging faculty, and replaced our then twenty-one-inch, black and white unit with a color set. I discussed our next project with the family, and they all agreed that a 'Color TV for 603' (that was our house number) was easy to mentally think about when **TV** entered our mind.

Then it happened—our first TV win. Chris won a sixteen-inch, portable, black and white set for naming a duck in a children's contest. About three weeks later, I won a fourteen-inch portable TV in a local radio contest. That, too, was black and white. We now kidded one another and discussed that perhaps we were not concentrating on 'color' enough. We agreed to give **color** more thought.

The next opportunity that presented itself was a caption contest. In ten words, we were to tell what a baby was saying. One of the newspapers was sponsoring this contest for humor. The only prizes offered were color TVs and portable black and white sets. This time, I was so positive I would win.

Of course, I did, but alas, another black and white set. I refused to be discouraged by what one might consider a failure, and I would not give up. It got to be a big joke around the Hadsell house: 'Mother is color blind,' or 'She isn't color-conscious.' After two years of projecting for a color TV, I finally gave in and went out and bought a set. That really wasn't any fun. I know there are no failures, only a delay in results, but that delay was just flat-out taking too long!

The following January, my husband flew to California on business. He wanted me to accompany him so we could see some live TV shows. It sounded like great fun, and we did have a fun time over the weekend as we attended a number of live shows.

On Monday, while he was transacting business, I had a free day. I chose to go to the NBC Studios in hopes of having an opportunity to once again see or talk to Art Linkletter.

May I go off on a tangent and explain *why* I wanted to meet him again? The year we won the trip to Disneyland, I had extended my visit for a few days. A former neighbor had moved to sunny California and invited me to stay on, visit, and be her guest. Here was an opportunity to see some of the live TV shows.

I had watched the Art Linkletter Show on occasion and always found the program to be sincere, wholesome, and entertaining. I also had hopes of one day being on a program. (A characteristic of mine; I'm a show-off.)

NOTE: I can only imagine what Helene's antics would have been like had YouTube or TikTok been around in her day.

My friend was able to acquire tickets. The night before I was to visit the studio and watch the show in progress, I suddenly had a very strong desire to be ON the show. While sleeping, I had a dream. It was quite vivid: Mr. Linkletter chose me from a vast audience and invited me to be on his program. (Most interesting because that is exactly how it happened.)

After the audience was seated, prior to the program, I was waiting for my dream to unfold in reality. Mr. Linkletter came on stage, looked over the audience, and walked up to where I sat, and amid hundreds of people present in the auditorium that day, he asked me, "Don't I know you?"

I guess I was speechless for a moment because it was happening just like I had seen it in my dream. What an unreal feeling.

"No, this is my first trip to Hollywood," I replied. He asked if I would like to have a very special Christmas present. "Sure," I replied. I was then escorted into the spotlight, and a huge box was placed before me. I was to open it so home viewers, and the audience could see my present. Well, it was quite a surprise. (No, it wasn't a color TV.) When I raised the lid, out jumped a little ol' Santa Claus, which scared the YELL out of me. After regaining my composure, jack-out-of-the-box presented me with a beautiful watch. The program was aired on Christmas Day, so all of my family and friends were able to witness my TV debut.

I was now a celebrity, so I didn't have to wish for that BIG DEAL anymore. After the program, Mr. Linkletter came to where I was seated and again asked if I was sure we had never met before that day. Now, you don't think I told him I dreamt about this. Of course, I didn't. Since that episode, I have done quite a bit of research and reading on telepathy, projection in dreams, regression into past lives, experiences of ancestors, etc.

I thought it would be interesting to get Mr. Linkletter's views on the subject. I, however, did not have the opportunity during my last visit. Perhaps, one day, I might have the occasion. I hope so.

Now, let's pick up the story that I was sharing with you earlier about visiting the NBC Studio. While taking the studio tour, I noted a line forming at the side of the building. People were waiting to be admitted into the studio to view a show being taped.

I asked how I could be admitted and found myself in line with the waiting group. The name of the show was It's Your Bet. They were going to shoot five half-hour programs that day. The following week, they would air them, one each day. One could be eligible for prizes if, number one; you were chosen by the camera that zoomed into the audience and stopped on you; number two, if the celebrity that was playing the game (it was sort of like ESP) could, in sequence, correctly answer three questions his mate had already submitted to the MC who was conducting the show. It's like the TV show called The Newlywed Game. If all the answers were correctly given by the game participant, the audience player would receive the prize that was flashed on the board prior to the game. It could be a refrigerator, color TV, washer, etc., but it would be a major appliance.

If they missed one, the prize would be of considerably lesser value: a portable appliance. If none were answered correctly, that would be your prize: nothing.

It sounded interesting, and certainly, it was a challenge—fun, fun. I had nothing to do until 5:00 PM. when I was to meet my husband.

While waiting, I became acquainted with a mother and her daughter, who were standing in line ahead of me. They began discussing the possibility of being chosen for one of the prizes. They were familiar with the program, and I was not. They informed me that they had been entering contests for years and had yet to win one prize. *"Bite your tongue, Helene,"* an inner voice said. *"Don't blow until you can show."* It suggested.

As I listened to their stories of failure, I realized why they hadn't won. It was obvious. Sure, they <u>wanted</u> to win, but instead of being positive, they had doubt. Not negation or pessimism, but just enough doubt that they nullified any positive energy they might have had when they entered a contest.

I call your attention to this because this is what most people are guilty of doing. They say they are positive, but somehow they don't retain this powerful energy constantly—until their wishes or desires manifest.

Here was the perfect opportunity for a positive experiment. I wanted these lovely people to win their desires. The mother wanted a color TV, and the daughter expressed a desire for a new refrigerator. It was only then that I turned on full-blast my concepts of how great I thought positive thinking was and asked if they would like to play a game using positive thinking and visualization. They agreed, but I could sense they were thinking, "What have we here, a kook?"

In all fairness, I must admit the studio audience was not too large: as an estimate, I would say about forty-five to fifty people. So that was cutting the odds considerably. I told them to be passive and not to project any positive energy until the item they wanted was flashed on the screen. When that happened, they were to know (think) they would be chosen by the house camera to vie for the prize and be the winner. They agreed.

After being chosen, I suggested they look at the answers given by the partner playing the game, then mentally project that answer to the person that was to give the correct answer. In other words, simply play mental telepathy. I reassured them several times it was a game, and if the three of us followed the rules, they would win the prizes. "What have you got to lose? It will make watching the game more interesting," I continued to explain.

Then the fun and games began. The first prize, which was projected on the board, was a silver service with an assortment of wine and a year's supply of wine. We knew that was not wanted, so we showed no concern. The next prize for the person in the audience to win was a color TV. I could see both of them perk up. The next minute, the house camera zoomed in on the mother. You better believe she was startled. She turned to give me a weak smile as if saying, "Well, I'll be." The players on the stage did their part. I'm sure both mother and daughter sent the answers to the person playing, and of course, I did. All three questions were answered correctly.

The bewitched, bothered, and bewildered homemaker from Ohio won her first prize: a color TV. The games went on, and prizes of no importance were offered. We were then informed there would be an hour break for lunch. The show would be continued after lunch. Three more programs would have to be taped. The three of us went across the street for a bite to eat. That is when the daughter asked the question; I knew she was quite concerned about it. Didn't I think the whole thing was just a coincidence? I agreed that it certainly did seem that way. So, would she like to now win her refrigerator by coincidence? "Why yes, let's do it again," she replied.

When we returned to the studio, the crowd had tripled in size. When she observed this, one could sense she was concerned. Then she gave me a weak smile and relaxed. The first prize that flashed on the screen for the audience was her refrigerator. The person that the camera zoomed in on was none other than the surprised daughter.

When the mental telepathy game began, it was amusing how swiftly the players picked up the answers. And, of course, she was the winner of the refrigerator. Well, what do you know, another coincidence? Perhaps. The only thing with me is, I flat never did believe in coincidences or accidents.

After that show was taped and completed, we had a ten-minute break before the next one would start. The mother and daughter asked me what I would like to win. They assured me that they would help me. At that time, I was having so much fun helping with their projects; I already had my reward. They left.

I still had two hours to spend before meeting my husband, so I stayed to continue watching the game.

As I sat in the audience, I could sense the group. Not one, to my sensing, had a strong desire to win an appliance.

Maybe they didn't need it; who knows? But I got restless and bored until I remembered that my dear old mother had mentioned, several times in her letters, that someday, she would like to have a color TV.

So here I go again. The camera zoomed in on me. The correct answers were sent to the players. I will admit that I got a little concerned for a moment when one of the players was wanting to give the wrong answer. (Sigh.) He paused, and then came forth with the right one. Thanks to the lovely people on the panel, my mother was able to enjoy a color TV.

"Why, that's witchcraft," some of you might be surmising. But of course, it's not. Let's call it what it really is: WISHcraft. But let's analyze this situation: the prizes were there for anyone who wished for them; the players of the game had free will—they could accept or reject anything that was mentally suggested to them.

Question: What if several people were vying for the same prize—which one would win?

Answer: The one that emitted the most positive energy.

Question: Can anyone do this?

Answer: It is being done every day, in every way. It's about time you are made aware of it.

When I became aware of the powerful tool one has when using their mind with control, I incorporated into my consciousness this phraseology: "*I will always use my power of the mind for constructive, creative purposes, for everything that is good, honest, constructive, and humanitarian. I will never use these powers of the mind for anything that is destructive or harmful to anyone.*" If that was my intention, I would not be able to function with these powers.

This I am most sincere about, for in my continuing research, I am aware that this powerful energy can be channeled for physical healings, to encourage the depressed, and can be of benefit to anyone who asks for help.

Several years ago, I happened to read a quote expressed by a man named Frank Outlaw. I would like to share his words with you now.

"Watch your thoughts, they become words; watch your words, they become actions; watch your actions, they become habits; watch your habits, they become character, watch your character, for it becomes your destiny."

NOTE: This was Helene's favorite quote. Write it out and stick it to your bathroom mirror or fridge. Read it daily for a reminder that one small thought now, especially when repeated, leads to your final destiny.

YES, YES YOU CAN

I'm curious to find out if a pooped couple with three kiddos can recapture the rapture of Springtime ecstasy in their fat, forty, frustrated years?

This is the entry I submitted in every contest that was offering a trip to Europe. I'd set my sights to fly high and vie for a trip to Paris, France.

I began 'Project Paris' the first of the year. I was anticipating celebrating my 40th birthday in Paris: I would be forty years old the first of June that year.

Back as far as I can remember, I had heard how picturesque, romantic, and exciting Paris was; sidewalk cafes, music, and relaxed, friendly, happy people. That is what prompted me to write the above entry. I wanted to go see for myself.

Of course, my husband would accompany me. You know it takes two, a he and a she.

I was really curious to find out if one could recapture the rapture of Springtime ecstasy in the city of life, love, and the pursuit of something!

I realize now that anything one does is based on what one thinks; how much daydreaming or energy one projects towards their goal. In fairness, I must admit, at the time of my Project Paris, I was impressed and influenced by all the things I'd heard and read about it. So, I had already halfway convinced myself it could happen. Now all I needed was to get my body there to experience in the flesh to see if the rapture could be recaptured.

I could go into a long declaration on what my idea of ecstasy means, but suffice it to say it's a carefree, comfortable, cozy, cool, calm, and protected feeling. That dear reader, is my idea of ecstasy.

A cola contest began shortly after the first of the year. It was just the contest I had been watching for. Top prizes were trips to anywhere in the world you wanted to go, and the promotion layout had this question: "Where in the world do you want to go and why?"

I knew I wanted to go to Paris, and I knew why I wanted to go. I *knew* I was going to Paris.

I was not too concerned about which contest would make this possible. Perhaps it would come in the form of a sum of money, but this time I would wait until my target date of May 15th, and then purchase tickets.

When you win trip prizes, they usually are package deals and must be accepted and taken by the winner.

I was not too concerned where in Europe any contest would take us because once I was in Europe, there would be no problem flying to Paris. So, I decided I would enter every contest until I won, and I had six months to make this dream a reality.

I'd read someplace that the stronger your faith, the more power you have. Also, you should continue to use your 'God-power' within you since you then acquire more power. *"You do not use up God-power,"* the statement said. *"It is inexhaustible, like the air we breathe."*

In recent years, I have been asked a number of times by students following the Eastern philosophy and vying toward spiritual growth if I didn't feel I was misusing 'God-power' for material things. Also, they claimed that if I continued to use the power, I would lose it.

My answer to this question must come from my experience. I do not believe it is a misuse of mental power to desire material things. Nor do I feel that it is 'God's Will' to punish anyone with pain, disease, and poverty. Perhaps I have a different God than people who have this belief. To my way of thinking, I like the phrase: **"Ask, and you shall receive, knock, and it shall be opened unto thee; seek and you shall find."** I have yet to come across any restrictions that limit you by saying, *"But don't ask for a trip, health, or a better job."*

If your way of thinking puts a damper on this type of goal or desire, then, dear reader, that is only your concept. I could write several novels on the misconceptions people have due to environment, religious dogma, guilt feelings, and set ways in their thinking, but I do say, if they have reached a point of no return, and they ponder or look for reasons, they must surely come up with the fact that they must change their ways. To change your ways, you must change your thinking.

There I go again, sandwiching in a sermonette in one of my fun-and-game projects. My son keeps a soapbox available for when I become 'sermonette-ish.'

Now let's get on with Project Paris. I want you to know the cola contest to which I submitted my entry did not award me a trip to Paris. They did, however, present me with a third prize, a Hammond Electric Organ. I did some serious thinking on that win. Here is the explanation as to why I feel I may have prompted the organ win.

Judges are nice people. Some are serious, some possess humor, and some have sympathy. I base this on the type of entries I've submitted and won in the past. One can sometimes write sad, glad, bad, and sometimes a little mad.

When the judges in the cola contest read my entry, I'm sure they found originality, the aptness of thought, and clarity of presentation, or it would not have been considered one of the top major prizes. However, I feel when it came to the final judging, the group talked it over and was concerned I might be a bit mad or disappointed if they sent me to Paris and I didn't 'recapture the rapture.' Perhaps they surmised what I really needed was therapy, and what better way to get it than to play the organ? Could this be the reason why they awarded me the organ? I'll never know, but I can guess, can't I?

Now surely you don't think I was disappointed. Remember earlier, I had said there is never a failure, only a delay in results. This is how I felt about this contest.

As I stated, there are many contests going on all the time, but I was only interested in trips to Europe or cash award contests, so I continued to enter.

The next contest that interested me was sponsored by a men's sportswear company. They were only offering six prizes: six trips to major cities in Europe. The rules were to complete, in twenty-five words or less, what city you would like to go to.

I again submitted that I wanted to go to Paris and why. I also submitted another entry that I wanted to go to Venice, Italy. It was beyond Paris, and prize-wise; it was the best deal one could win. The trip was first class, but only for one person.

It was now May 1st of that year, and we still had not heard of any trip I'd won. I'd won a number of minor prizes but no trip. We did get our shots and passports, and we also questioned what was taking somebody, somewhere, so long to notify us.

Several days later, our son, Chris, won a trip to New York for two. We were quite elated as we realized New York is halfway to Europe from Texas. We did not have much time left for my June 1st target date.

It was a week later when we got the telegram from the men's sportswear contest. My husband had won the trip to Venice; he could leave immediately if he wished.

We did some fast *wheelin' 'n' dealin'*, changing the first-class ticket to tourist class, and we were actually refunded money from the airline after booking passage for two. It worked beautifully.

Chris, my husband, and I flew to New York. We spent three days at the World's Fair and, from there, went on to Europe after we sent Chris on a plane back to Texas.

It was June 1st when my husband and I were seated at the sidewalk cafe in Paris, sipping wine.

Now I want all of you to know, YES, you can recapture the rapture of springtime ecstasy, although fat, forty, and frustrated.

When our exciting trip (three weeks in length) to the enchanting cities in Europe came to a close, I again felt thirty, pretty, and flirty. It's a state of mind. I agree. Please don't knock it until you try it.

Now, Act Surprised, They Expect It

Little did I realize what was in the 'making for taking' when I went to the contest club meeting after my return from Europe.

The group met on the first Monday in September, shortly after I returned from my European tour.

I was now known as 'The Gad About,' with the many trips I'd won in the contesting field. I might add I also was 'glad about' the many comforts and conveniences provided by the merchandise prizes I had won.

"Can you top this?" seemed to be the question that now presented itself.

After I shared my trip experience with the members present, everyone expressed a desire that they, too, might like to win a trip to Europe.

When the announcement was made of current contests now in progress, I really perked up when I heard that the Formica Company was awarding a dream home in their building material promotion. Now to me, that could be <u>The Livin' Beginning</u>.

The Formica home that someone would win had been on display at the New York World's Fair. I must admit, although I attended the fair, I was not aware of the contest nor their display. Perhaps I was too excited about our European tour.

The contest was promoting Formica products.

All home builders in the USA, who built a home with a certain amount of Formica products, and who participated in the Parade of Homes had the entry blanks and the rules.

In order to participate in the contest, the rules specified you had to be a family homeowner, and you must have visited one of the

55

Formica homes participating in the contest. This was Monday evening, and the deadline was on Friday of the following week.

I was told that the only Formica home participating in our area that had blanks for the contest was in Garland, Texas, nineteen miles from Irving.

On the way home from the club meeting that evening, I kept thinking of the house—all new, modern, and spacious. The more I thought about it, the better I liked the idea. It was made to order for me.

Tuesday morning, when I woke up, all I thought about was the house. After my husband left for work and the children were off to school, I tried to get on with my daily tasks. Call it a hunch, intuition, or WISHcraft; I felt compelled to drive to Garland to register in the sweepstakes.

It began to rain. I called a friend who also enjoys entering contests and happens to live in Irving. I asked her to drive to Garland with me to register.

"Sorry, I can't go Helene. I just washed my hair, and it's a miserable day to be on the highway," she said. I called another friend in hopes she might go with me. No, she was sewing and didn't want to get out in the rain. She reminded me that the contest promotion had been on for almost two years, and it was a waste of gas and time at this late date. I then tried to bribe her into going with me by telling her I would buy her a pizza for lunch. No luck!

Next, I tried to talk myself out of going until later in the week, but I certainly did not dismiss the idea of entering. Somehow, the most important thing for me to do that day was to get in the car, drive to Garland, and register my name for that home.

NOTE: Helene took inspired action. If you have a gut feeling or hunch to go in a particular direction, do a specific task, etc. DO IT! It is your intuition guiding you, even if it seems illogical. Everyone has had experiences in their life when they have ignored it and regretted that decision.

I drove in the rain, located the Formica home, and registered both my name and my husband's name. I then sat in the spacious living room as I admired the beautiful furnishings and master craft workmanship of the Formica features.

It was then I became aware that I would win the house. Don't ask me how. I just **KNEW**.

I took an entry blank home and was re-reading the rules when I pushed the panic button. I'd signed my husband's name, and the rules stated the winner must have visited one of the Formica homes. He hadn't.

When he got home that evening, I insisted that he drive to Garland with me and familiarize himself with the house, so when the judges notified us, we would not be disqualified by not following the rules. I learned that you could lose a major prize by goofing up and not following the rules.

I know a woman who entered a contest to win a five-room house of furniture. She really wanted and needed the prize because they were then building a new home. She signed her eleven-year-old daughter's name to the entry she submitted. She was so interested in keying her entry to find out what she had written that might win; she didn't follow the rules that stated you must be an adult. When the judging firm called, and the daughter answered and told the judges she was eleven years old, that was the end of that.

The mother later called the agency to explain she hadn't noticed the contest was for adults over twenty-one years of age. The judges were sorry she overlooked the rule, but they had to abide by the rule as the furniture company sponsoring the contest would not award their top prize to a child.

That same weekend, we drove to Garland, introduced ourselves to the builder, and reviewed the details of the house. When we returned home, my great expectations began to manifest. Active faith alone will impress the subconscious, and I wasn't going to miss a beat.

The following week, I decided the house would be furnished with hand-carved Spanish furniture. Why not? I'd seen just what I wanted on one of our trips to Mexico. I asked my husband to draw up plans for the house. The boys also put in their wants and desires. They suggested we have a huge game room, one that would accommodate a full-size pool table, the organ we had won earlier, the TV center and music area, and several couches for informal entertaining. I expressed the desire that the kitchen and breakfast area be open to the patio garden. We got so specific we were all projecting toward its reality.

Our next act of faith was to spend weekends looking at lots for the house to be built on. The rules stated we could choose a lot anywhere in the United States, and Formica would pay for the lot, too. We spotted three lots that would suit our purpose. We had a fun time on this project alone.

Six weeks passed, and still no news. Then one evening, while I was attending a club meeting, the phone rang. My husband was there to answer it.

The judging firm that was handling the contest promotion was calling. No, not to say that we have won any prize, just to ask questions. The formal procedure is to see if contestants followed all the rules.

Question: Was H. B. Hadsell married and a homeowner?

Question: Did we visit a Formica home, and where?

Of course, my husband could answer all the questions because we had followed the rules.

This preliminary investigation does not mean that you have won the prize. We were informed this is necessary to avoid awarding top prizes to people who are not eligible because they hadn't followed all the rules. The company also must be certain that there is such a person and that they are not related to anyone working for the company or conducting the contest.

NOTE: Always read the official rules. Every clause. This practice has not stopped. With modern technologies, potential big winners are investigated and vetted behind the scenes by detective agencies before being declared potential winners. You agree to this search when you agree to abide by the official rules. It's only after all the release forms are signed that you are then declared an official winner.

We were excited after the investigation and now questioned ourselves as to how long it would take them to make it official that we were the winners of their house.

A week later, on Friday morning, to be exact, I announced that we would hear of our house win today. I recall commenting on how I'd better get the house straightened up in case the officials came early. Also, I'd have to make a trip to the bakery to get pastries to serve these lovely people. My husband decided to stay home from work that day so that he could be on hand for the big moment.

At 3:00 PM, the phone rang. The person on the other end of the line identified himself as one of the 'big wheels' from Formica. Heavens, no, he didn't refer to himself as a 'big wheel,' but logic will tell you they certainly would not send a 'nobody' for a big deal like awarding a dream house. He was accompanied by a public relations man, whom I can only refer to as a ball-of-fire and a showy individual. I really liked the fellow because it's the live wires that get a job done.

The 'big wheel' asked if he and one of his associates (the ball of fire) might come to our home to discuss a contest prize for which we were being considered. "If your husband is not home this time of day, we will wait until later in the evening, as we wish to have both of you present," he explained.

I almost blew it. I was about to blurt out, "What took you so long?" Instead, I answered, "Oh, do come on out. My husband is home today, and I have the coffee perkin'."

"NOW ACT SURPRISED, THEY EXPECT IT!" was the instruction I gave my husband. They came. We did.

When the glad tidings were verbally made official, the merry-go-round began. They informed us that there had been over two million entries for that sweepstakes.

It took no time to get the home ready for the show. They approved the lot, selected the architect, and incorporated our wishes into the house plans.

The Formica team, the builder, and everyone connected with the Hadsell house were wonderful. They did so many nice 'added things' to please us.

Now, every time I see any Formica products, I again mentally thank this team of lovely people for turning our wishes into reality.

"What about taxes?" is the first question people seem to ask.

Formica thought about that, too. They informed us that if there were any financial concerns over taxes, they would help us with this so we would not be burdened by turmoil or taxes and turn against this good fortune. However, we were able to take care of the situation, and for the past years, we've enjoyed our spacious, gracious, comfortable Formica fortress.

One of the nicest features of this beautiful home was the 'carefreedomness' of work, worry, and waxing. Formica took care of us, and now Formica takes care of itself.

Beautiful people, are you beginning to realize the power of positive thinking and active faith?

Change your expectations, and you change your conditions. Begin to act as if you expect success, happiness, and abundance. PREPARE FOR YOUR GOOD. Nothing is too good to be true; nothing is too wonderful to happen; nothing is too good to last when you have a positive attitude for your good.

How to Be Successful Without Really Trying

There is never any failure. Only a delay in results.
Helene Hadsell

The following are a number of personal experiences to again, relay what can happen when the ideas of security, health, happiness, and abundance are firmly established in the subconscious.

It means a life free from all limitations! It surely must be the 'Kingdom' which Jesus spoke of, where all things are automatically added unto us because all life is vibration; the things which symbolize these states of consciousness will attach themselves to us.

In other words, 'Tune In.' Feel rich and successful, and suddenly you will receive a gift or a large sum of money.

My husband and I attended a company Christmas party where a door prize of a tape recorder would be presented in a drawing. Everyone in attendance had heard of our phenomenal success in winning things. One man, prior to the drawing, jokingly announced, "The Hadsells should be disqualified because no one can win when they enter a contest." Of course, we won the tape recorder, and we didn't even try.

Why did we win? Perhaps our past accumulation of positive energy had something to do with the win. I recall the incident quite clearly: when we were all aware what the door prize was, I simply expressed a desire that I might win it. We had intentions of getting one as a gift for one of the children.

For this incident, I have no logical explanation except to say, "T'was just plain ole WISHcraft."

If you should happen to be resentful and envious (and admit it to yourself), say this powerful, positive statement: "What God has done

63

for others, God now does for me and more." Repeat it until it becomes second nature in your consciousness; then, all the things you desire will come your way. Don't be discouraged if you have a desire and it does not produce results as swiftly as the tape recorder win. Remember, there is never any failure, only a delay in results. There, I said it again.

Over the years, I have learned not to be disappointed in anything, anyone, or any goal I project. If it does not manifest as fast as I might wish it, say, for example, had I not won the tape recorder, my attitude would have been: "Oh well, you win some, you lose some. I KNOW it was premature, but it is still coming to me."

Don't ever dismiss or nullify good, positive energy because you are disappointed. Acquire the attitude, "I guess I need a little more patience." It really does wonders for your peace of body, mind, and well-being. YOU WILL GET IT.

Somewhere I read this bit of advice that I find most appropriate: No man gives to himself, but himself, and no man takes away from himself, but himself: The Game of Success is a game of solitaire; as you change, all conditions will change.

MY SOW AND REAP PHILOSOPHY

Nine local automobile dealerships and super-market companies co-sponsored a contest.

To win, one had to go to the auto showroom to view the latest model car that was filled to capacity with groceries. The person that guessed closest to the amount of the total sum of the groceries would win a $150.00 coupon book, which could be spent in the stores. The second-closest guess would win the use of a sports car for a week.

When I heard of this contest, I called a friend and asked her if she would like to accompany me to play the guessing game to win some groceries.

We began our 'fun-and-games' day this way.

On our visit to the first dealer, we submitted our guesses and agreed that I had the correct sum and I would win the $150.00 prize in that dealership. At our next stop, we jokingly designated that my friend would win the cash award from that dealer, the next place I would win, and the next one she would win.

I must repeat again; we were in a very happy mood and had great fun playing the game of guessing. There were four places where I would win the first prize and four places where she would win. When we came to the ninth dealer, she suggested, "Let's win for my neighbor who has five children and could really use the $150.00 grocery money." We submitted our guesses in her neighbor's name and concluded our fun-and-game day.

Winners would be announced on Saturday of that week. We decided to stay home that day to answer the phone, and we would call each other later that evening to check out our score.

One might say at this point, "This is unreal," but let me assure you it is fact.

I had three phone calls that afternoon. Two informed me that I had won their prize of a $150.00 coupon book. One told me I missed the total figure by three cents, but I won the second prize—the use of their sports car for a week. My friend won the $150.00 prize at two dealers, and the neighbor, whose name we submitted, also won the first prize of $150.00 from another dealer. The one dealer I hadn't heard from concerned me. I told my friend I had a hunch he was dishonest because I was certain I HAD SUBMITTED THE RIGHT AMOUNT at that dealership. The more I thought of it, the more I felt compelled to follow my hunch.

NOTE: Always follow your inner voice. It's not always easy as it is very quiet, but the more you practice, the better you get. Plus, you will discover even when it defies logic at the moment, in the end, it will turn out to be correct.

On Monday, I called the place and asked the secretary who answered the phone, "Who won the $150.00 grocery certificate book?" She told me the supervisor who was in charge of the promotion had taken care of that, and she felt the winner had already been notified.

I told her I would call back and speak to the supervisor, as I was most interested in who won the prize. Several hours later, I called again. This time I spoke to the man in charge. He informed me that the winner had been notified, but he forgot her name. It was somewhere on his desk, and he had a customer, so he had no time to look it up. I told him I would call back in an hour, as I was curious to find out who won. At this point, I felt certain that this man was dishonest, and I knew I would not drop the issue. When I called again, he curtly informed me that a woman living in Irving named Helene Hadsell had won. The car dealership was in Ft. Worth. "How wonderful. I know her," I quickly commented before I hung up. What choice did he now have but to follow through?

Two days later, in the mail, I received the prize of the coupon book, with a note of this nature: "We are pleased to inform you that you are the winner in our contest." The postmark on the envelope indicated it was mailed after my telephone conversation.

The moral of this experience is: I did not entertain any negative ideas about anyone being dishonest, but when the strong hunch prompted me to investigate, I did, and I was correct.

In my experience of contesting, I have had only two instances when I felt the person in charge was not honest. Both were in local promotions.

It is amusing to think about dishonesty, for "As you sow, so shall you reap." The more I become aware of this well-organized universe we live in, the more I realize the perfection of this law. You really don't kid anyone but yourself when you are dishonest. Although at one time, you may feel you have pulled a fast one, sometime in the future, someone will pull a fast one on you. This law was laid down for us centuries ago.

This raises the thought—perhaps you are reaping what you once sowed; perhaps the reason the prize was withheld is for this law to be balanced for one of the past shenanigans you pulled. This is very possible, but again, I could only follow my intuition and pursue the incident to my satisfaction or dismiss it as not worth the effort.

HUNCHES ARE THE HANDIEST THINGS

After we moved into our dream home, we had no reason to 'keep up with the Jones.' We were the Jones.

My son, Chris (the joker), at the time sixteen years old, called my attention to the fact that he, at long last, was in the surroundings he should have been accustomed to a long time ago. In other words, what took you so long? He now expressed a desire for a sports car, a 'sharp' new wardrobe, impressive rings, and things to show how prosperous he was. He wanted to create a new image. Okay, I'll say it: he was a showoff. Or should I chalk it up as being a teenager, and if you have ever been around one, nuf said on that subject.

What a difficult time the little darlings can sometimes make for themselves. It seems like no amount of love, patience, attention, and understanding can reach them during one period of the *growin', blowin', and showin'* syndrome.

Fortunately, this period is brief, and one can always be comforted in the fact this, too, will pass. Again, let me reassure you that there are never any failures, only a delay in results. There now, does that give you hope? Anyway, this was the period Chris was going through. That might give you further verification that we are the typical family, nutty as well as fruitful.

But let's get back to Chris' desire, the complete list of items he was vying for. Would you now believe a contest appeared on the scene that answered all his wants?

The Union Carbide Company was sponsoring a contest for teenagers. Rules called for the design of a piece of jewelry that would appeal to the youth. Requirements were to use one or more 'Linde Star Sapphires' on the piece of jewelry you designed. The Company was plugging star sapphires.

I understood the contest had been in progress for almost six months, and all art classes in schools throughout the USA were informed and encouraged to submit their ideas. There were two first prizes, one for a girl and one for a boy. The big first prize included a trip to New York for a week to attend the national jewelry show. One parent could accompany their 'genius-child,' jewelry-designer winner. A star sapphire ring would be presented to the winner, as well as a gold wristwatch, two pieces of luggage, a $1,000 cash award, plus a trip to the men's manufacturing firm to choose a fall wardrobe of your choice. Now I ask you, how does that grab you for having 'all your begs in one ask-it'? I mean, 'all your eggs in one basket.' Don't you see, that contest was geared for Chris?

It was about the last week before the contest closed when he got all fired up about entering. What kind of entry wins, and what did he submit? The following are the incidents that led up to his win.

He discussed the ideas of the contest with the whole family and came up with this: nearly everyone in high school at that time was either in a band or combo or thought they could play a musical instrument of some sort. He first toyed with the idea of submitting a banjo but, after giving it more thought, discarded it. He felt it was too obvious—most of his friends were talking about the banjo those days—and it might not be original enough. He maintained the musical idea, and then the thought came: why not a staff with two notes and a treble clef?

That would be a great idea for a tie bar and would appeal to all the teenagers. Although the rules did not call for you to title the piece of jewelry you designed, he figured he would call it the LINDE GO GO. It was a natural for his entry. He was so excited that he immediately sat down and drew his idea on paper.

He was not artistically inclined, nor was he an art student, but that was not a specific requirement. It included all high-school students. His enthusiasm was now on high. Then he yelled out, "I just had another great idea," as he headed for the garage and tool chest. He came back a few minutes later with a pair of pliers and a flexible piece of wire... He then commenced shaping the wire into a staff. He then made another trip for finer wire to depict the lines where the notes would be placed. He puzzled for a minute over what might be suitable to represent the star sapphire that would be incorporated into the jewelry. He headed for the pantry and looked at the dried rice and bean assortment I had. He decided on two small dried peas. He then glued the whole thing together, and sprayed it gold, except the peas, which he left a pale green. I don't mind boasting a bit here because we were all quite proud of his workmanship and *WINgenuity*.

Although the contest called for a drawn sketch, which he did, he also felt compelled to mail in his 'paste-up' idea. He mounted it in a jewelry box lined with black velvet, and it looked quite impressive

As far as I was concerned, he already had a prize for the amount of pleasure he derived from his creativity.

After he mailed in his entry, I was excited about going to New York again. I bought a pale lemon-colored suit for our trip and shopped for new accessories as I waited for the judges to notify him that he had won the first prize.

On Monday, about two weeks after the contest closed, I woke up with the strong hunch that today would be the day we would hear from the jewelry design contest.

I was so positive; I would have made a small bet on it happening. The mailman came with no news in the mail, but that didn't discourage me. There could still be news forthcoming via telephone or wire.

NOTE: Companies rarely call or mail you to notify you that you are a prize winner. The most popular ways to contact contest winners today are via email, text, social media tag, or direct message.

We had planned on going shopping sometime that day to get Chris a pair of shoes. We had to do it before 5:00 PM, as he went to baseball practice at that time. Somehow, I kept postponing leaving the house as if I was stalling for time. Then the phone rang shortly after 4:00 PM. It was one of the judges from New York. Chris answered the phone. They informed him that they only had one question to ask, "Was Chris a girl or a boy?" His answer was, "I am all boy." The next morning, we received the wire that Chris had won first prize for his jewelry design entry.

My hunch paid off by staying home until the phone call, as we later learned.

While we were in New York, enjoying the prizes, praises, and fabulous places, the lovely public relations people took us to meet the judges. (This was after the prize had been awarded.) They wanted to meet the two top teenage designers.

One of the judges, a woman, explained how difficult it was in making the top award selections. She told us that there was no question about the girl winner, but the final judging of the top teen boy entry proved a challenge. The final decision was between a boy named Mike, who, incidentally, submitted a banjo design as his entry, and Chris for a musical staff presentation. When the nitty-gritty time came to select one winner, the judges were tired after several days of studying all the entries, and it was still a tie between Chris and Mike. The woman judge wanted Chris to win because she was so impressed that anyone would take the extra trouble to submit an actual paste-up. The male judges tried to get her to agree with them and give Mike the prize. They were certain Mike was a boy. They were concerned that if they awarded it to Chris, and Chris was a girl, they would have two girl winners.

So, they did have a consideration. The woman judge said she finally agreed to complete the judging, but on one condition. She insisted that they call this kid from Texas. "If he answers the phone and tells us he is a boy, he gets the prize. If no one answers, I will concede that Mike is the winner." They agreed as they wanted to conclude their judging that afternoon.

Well, Chris was home, he answered the phone, he is a boy, and he was the winner.

This incident again should convince you that when you have a hunch, and it makes sense, follow it. In my personal experience, it pays off ten out of ten times.

What an opportunity that was for Chris. From desiring to acquiring his wishes took only four weeks.

This prize win and experience were two more of the Hadsell's highlights.

THE SUPREME TEST

Now just what makes you think I should limit my positive thinking to contest wins? I admit I had my beginning with the will-to-win-contests goal, but then something exciting happened to open a whole new concept for me.

It was shortly after we moved into the house. At the insistence of one of my friends, we drove to Fort Worth to hear a man speak from Laredo, Texas. His name was José Silva. Mr. Silva was lecturing on the power of the mind. He told us how one could control habits, weight, sleep without drugs, and a lot of other good things. His 48-hour course included techniques of mental imagery for better health, better memory, superior intuition, and productivity, as well as how one could control pain. The man was so sincere, and as I listened to him explain one's mind potential, I knew I had to take this course. Why, I got so excited I could hardly wait until the following evening to begin class training. That, dear reader, was the best investment I have ever made to date. Four months after completing the SILVA MIND DEVELOPMENT course, I had the occasion to give the techniques I had been taught by José Silva the supreme test.

My husband and I were involved in an automobile accident one evening on a slick, sleet-covered bridge. My face was thrown against the dashboard as the car hit us head-on. The impact flattened my nose, caused internal facial damage, and I was unable to breathe due to the great amount of blood I was swallowing. I had two choices, to push the panic button and bleed to death or stop the bleeding.

Dear reader, let me now confess that in the past, I probably was one of the most difficult patients who the medical profession ever treated. I went into hysterics at the sight of blood. Just going to the hospital to visit a friend made me sick to my stomach; perhaps I sensed the fear and pain. I also had so many of my own fears of dying, sickness, and pain that I frankly could have been labeled a prize neurotic.

Seems every time I heard some person relate their experiences of surgery or pain; I incorporated it into my consciousness, HOOK, LINE, AND THINKER.

Let's get on with the accident experience because WOW! was I fortunate. When it occurred, I was clued in on how to handle the situation, thanks to the Silva Mind Development program. One of the techniques we were taught in the course was to stop and control bleeding, plus how to control pain.

I immediately demanded the bleeding to stop, and you know what? It did. At this point, the medical doctor would claim, and rightly so, that our body has a survival mechanism that triggers and aids us to respond to survive. I agree. But when one possesses a powerful imagination along with fear, it overrides any physiological response that would react, and one can (and many times does) bleed to death or die of shock caused by fear and panic. I could have been one of those statistics had it not been for the Silva Mind Development techniques to stop the bleeding.

After thirty-five minutes of being in the car until help arrived, I was placed in an ambulance with the sirens on all the way to the hospital's emergency room. I questioned why the BIG RUSH, for the events that followed, were a farce.

After being wheeled into the emergency room for incoming patients, I lay on a cold table for an hour or more while papers were signed until my turn came for a 'look at.' I kept my eyes closed since the floodlights I was directly under were so intense. Finally, two staff members came to view my broken body. One had this to say, "I wonder what she looked like?"

I tell you this not to belittle the hospital system because I'm sure the staff only does what it is trained to do. I hope this will help you handle a situation if you ever happen to be in a similar circumstance. I hope you never are.

Again, I had a chance to feel sorry for myself, rant, rave, moan, and groan, or control the situation by thinking positive (another supreme test). I began my mental musings with constructive, creative thinking. "I will be fine; why with the remarkable plastic surgery I hear they are now doing, I know they can improve on my looks. This body will heal itself so fast; my medical case history will be a miracle for its speedy recovery." Over and over, I mentally told myself the above positive suggestions.

The diagnosis of the injuries sustained from the accident after the complete once-over, twice-over, three times-over (I must say once they got around to examining me, they were most thorough) there were: fractured ribs in the lower back, bruised spleen, right ankle swollen three times the normal size. They could find no reason for this as there was no fracture visible on the X-ray. Immediate surgery to reconstruct my nose and repair facial damage was recommended. I was given sodium pentothal to undergo face and nose surgery.

The prognosis for the damage and injury in the back, ribs, and ankle would be six weeks of limited activity in a wheelchair, plus wearing a corset for back support.

After the facial surgery, and upon regaining consciousness, I woke up to a room full of friends who came to bring healing energy.

77

People truly are beautiful. One of my friends, a former registered nurse, insisted on just sitting beside my bed as she claimed she could sense my physical needs.

She would administer to my needs until the anesthetic wore completely off, and I was in control and rational.

After my system was free of the drugs administered for surgery, I never had another shot or pain pill during the two weeks I remained in the hospital. I didn't need it. When I was aware of discomfort, I merely 'conned' myself by imagining the throbs of pain (that I was once so fearful of) were healing pulsations. With each awareness of the throbbing sensation, I mentally repeated, "Healing, healing, healing."

This is interesting as it was the first time I realized the throbbing sensation that is called pain, comes in cycles and isn't constant. I also was aware that when I used the technique of physical relaxation, which I was taught in the Silva Class, the intensity of the throbbing was very mild. I now had changed pain cycles to positive healing cycles; there was no more pain, only pleasant healing pulsations.

Ah-ha, I sense doubt in some of you readers.

This is to be expected, for prior to my Mind Development Training, I, too, had been a big doubter. Some of you might call this technique self-hypnosis, programming, or plain stupidity since drugs were available to keep me knocked out. But I will say, not one of you can say it doesn't work because I'm here to tell you it did, and it does.

I must keep telling you the power of the mind is fantastic. I'm sure some of you are aware of the fire walkers who walk over hot coals and do not get burned, nor do they feel discomfort, or of the people that are human pin-cushions and feel no pain as pins are stuck in their bodies. They have conditioned and disciplined themselves with their thinking to such a degree that they actually refuse pain. They are not special people. I certainly am not special. We all have this ability to control feelings, pain, or environments and our lives. Don't limit yourself for this works in all capacities.

BIG QUESTION MARK: "But I haven't had any mental training, so how does one develop this powerful, positive attitude you're talking about?" In the chapter SPEC I will give you a step-by-step plan for positive thinking results. Remember, you must first have the desire to be master of your mind.

Scientists tell us that we are using less than ten percent of our mind power. I believe it is because, as I continue to study mind power, I am amazed at what one is capable of doing by right or by wrong thinking.

My healing was what one might term a 'miracle.' When I was released from the hospital and back at home, the wheelchair came right home with me. Of course, it served a useful purpose. I looked at it as it sat in the corner while I took over my household activities.

I thought, "I am not an invalid. I am in complete control of my body. My body does not control me. I control my body." And boy, did it straighten up and perform!

I was requested to check with the doctor who did the face surgery and the doctor who was tending to my back and leg injury. I really didn't want to go, but it was required by the doctors for other reports to collect fees from the accident insurance company.

I first went to the surgeon, who did such a fine job of rebuilding my nose. He was about to probe, and 'nose around' and check his workmanship by inserting a metal object up my nose when I rebelled. I told him I was quite happy with my nose job. I felt great. It had healed perfectly, and I had no further need for wasting his time or my time. Yes, I was rude, and I'm sure I hurt his pride by being so abrupt. My policy to always "leave 'em laughing, loving, loyal, and lucky to know me" was a BUST. I goofed miserably, so I had no choice but to make amends.

I have always been proud of having a sense of humor (although sometimes my husband disagrees with me and tells me that my humor doesn't make sense). Nevertheless, I spent the next day trying to compensate for my rude behavior during my visit to the good doctor. I hoped that he might have a sense of humor, so I pulled out my crayons. (I keep them on hand for my grandchildren when they come for a 'getting into everything' session.) I drew a beautiful picture of my nose. I then composed a citation which I typed and attached under the drawing of the nose. I then framed the entire masterpiece and titled it: AWARD OF MERIT FOR DR. (and inserted his name). The citation read as follows: "After extensive nosin' around getting this thing back in runnin' condition, I am most appreciative. You have not only performed a humanitarian duty, you have definitely improved upon my beauty. All that now remains is paying through it." Then I signed my name.

Perhaps my husband was right when he said my sense of humor sometimes doesn't make sense, for I promptly received a bill for his services, and I haven't seen or heard from the dear boy since. To the readers who are inclined to agree with my husband's view that my humor doesn't make sense, that's fine. But give me credit on this score—I may be a nut, but you can bet I'll never be in a rut.

WINEUVERS FOR WISHCRAFT

"I knew I was going to win," said the winner of a $10,000 first-prize cash award.

So the news came as no surprise when the Dallas woman answered her doorbell, and two representatives of an advertising agency were there to present her with a check for $10,000.

The story began last summer when the woman told two of her best friends, "This is going to be my year. My whole life is going to change. I feel it, I KNOW IT."

Just what did she do to accomplish this WIN-fall? Why she used her power of positive thinking.

In her words, she summed it up this way. "If you just open your heart and believe in good things, they are bound to happen. You simply train your mind to believe and to hope until it happens."

Her goal was not for $10,000. Actually, it was for $5,000. She also had three things she wanted to accomplish for the year.

"I needed a new car; I wanted to establish a home again with a good husband; I play the organ at my church, but I've never owned one of my own, and have always wanted one, so I could play at home; and lastly, I wanted a little financial security, and felt that $5,000 would be ample," she related.

"I made a 'wheel of fortune,' a simple circular piece of cardboard with cut-out pictures tacked to it. There were pictures of a new automobile, a couple holding hands (depicting happiness), an electric organ, and a nest with an egg representing the $5,000: I boldly printed the sum of $5,000 on the egg. I put the wheels (because I actually made four) in places where I would be constantly reminded of my goals and could give them energy continuously. All that remained was for them to materialize," she laughed.

One of her wheels of fortune was placed on her TV; another on the dash of her car; the other in her desk drawer at work; and the other on her nightstand, as they would be the last thing she would think about before falling asleep.

With all those reminders, it was a constant process of sending energy out. It's a good idea because that's better than thinking of aches and pains or feeling sorry for yourself. In some schools of thought, it is called being single-minded. Within a few weeks, she was able to buy a new car. "It was a deal I couldn't turn down. Why it was almost like a gift," she explained. She then removed the picture of the car from her wheel of fortune.

For one of the church programs, a traveling gospel quartet presented the program. She was attracted to one of the members, and they found they had a lot in common. Several months later, he returned to Dallas, left the quartet, took a job locally, and they got married. Another picture was removed.

It was in May, on her birthday, when her husband presented her with an organ for their home. Three down, one to go.

"He knew of my projects. In fact, he got a kick out of it. But he said, 'Okay, kid, I was number two for you, but I can't imagine how or where you will get a lump sum of $5,000.'"

"It was the second week in June when I was notified; I won not $5,000, but the first prize of $10,000 in a sweepstakes. I'd seen the ad for the contest in a magazine and mailed it in. I told myself at the time, here is where I can get my egg money."

All her dreams were realized within a year. The beauty of this true story is that we all have the capability, so let's discuss how one can accomplish this and how it works.

Do you know what you really want? Don't be too quick with your answer because the average person has so many wants, desires, and wishes. They change daily with one's moods. You are not able to give yourself the chance to generate enough energy for your end result if you vacillate.

I suggest you play this mental game with yourself. Ask yourself, *"What is the most important goal I wish to accomplish?"* Think about it seriously. Is it positive, constructive, and creative? Sort of imagine having it. Feel how it feels to have it. How will it change your lifestyle?

A word of advice. You need never involve another to obtain your end result. Imposing your will on others is a NO-NO and is really not necessary. Let me give you this example. You are working in an office position. Your boss is a fink, he goofs off, and there is only one way to do things, 'his way.' You feel he lacks the knowledge for this position, and you know you could do better. You want his job. You might entertain the idea that he gets fired, or the higher boss gets wise to him as you have, and at last, you get the position you should have had all along. Granted, we all fantasize about this type of situation at times. We dismiss it because our mind gets busy on other things.

What I'm saying is, if you kept up this thought long enough and strong enough for it to become an obsession, chances are that it would happen in due time. THIS IS NOT THE WAY TO PLAY THE GAME. You can obtain the same end results with peace of mind and not have to manipulate people. You can enjoy your achievements with this method: *"I desire the perfect job with perfect pay."* That is all: that is necessary. Every time your job comes to mind, repeat this phrase silently or think about it. With this as an end result, it will work its way to fruition in due course. Your boss may be transferred, resign, or whatever, or you may even be offered another job with another firm that may meet all your needs. There is no need to set things up; just watch how they all fall into place. For if this is truly your end result, and you use proper mental desire, you will accomplish it.

One of the finest publications that goes into detail on a plan to accomplish a goal is titled, *It Works: The Famous Little Red Book That Makes Your Dreams Come True!* by RHJ.

As I lecture throughout the United States, I get questions from the audience regarding particular situations. I also ask them if they wish to write and tell me their experiences of how they obtained their end result. The following is an incident that happened to a student.

"I don't enter contests, and I don't feel that I can afford the money out of the family budget for my desire," she said.

NOTE: At that time, the main method of entering sweepstakes was mail-in. You would need to buy paper, 3x5s, envelopes, pens, and stamps. Now, you do not have the expense of entering online giveaways as you most likely already own a computer and/or cell phone.

Her desire was to take a trip to the Bahamas. Seems like one of her friends had taken the leisure cruise and had related how great it was. It so impressed the student that she, too, wanted to make the voyage. Her husband, however, did not share her enthusiasm, nor did he care to go. That did not dampen her desire. She still wanted it for herself.

I suggested that she continue to project energy and know that her wish would come true. Four weeks later is when I received a postcard with a picture of a ship postmarked from the Bahamas. The card merely stated, *"I named it and am now claiming it,"* and her signature.

Upon her return home, she wrote me the details of how this all came about. While taking art classes, she got acquainted with one of the other students in her class. The student, who was a distributor for women's cosmetics, told the lady that the company she worked for was having a sales promotion, and the person in each district with the largest sales would win a trip to the Bahamas. She was confident she would win the trip. To date, she had submitted the largest amount of sales. That is when the student told her of her desire to take such a trip. The lady wished her artist friend success on her win and hoped that the trip would be all she had dreamed.

A week later, she received a phone call from the artist friend. She had won the trip and was ready to leave when her son suddenly became ill and had to undergo an appendectomy. She couldn't leave under these conditions, and she knew of no one in her family that could make or want the trip on such short notice. If it was not taken, it would be lost as it was a preplanned package deal. So, if she wanted the trip, it was hers, free, with no strings attached. Of course, she accepted and was elated because the experience was everything she had hoped for. She confessed that she was amazed at how quickly everything fell into place.

Recently, I met a woman in a shopping center in Dallas who recognized me. She had heard my lecture on 'WINeuvers for WISHcraft' and immediately applied the ideas. She had to share her success. She and her husband had just moved into a new home and were in the process of furnishing it. After hearing my lecture, she knew what her desire would be. She wanted a china cabinet just like her grandmother had. She recalled how she admired the piece of furniture whenever she visited her. When her grandmother passed away, her estate was sold and distributed, and no one seemed to know just where the china cabinet was. Nevertheless, her desire was to have the china cabinet or a duplicate placed against one wall in her breakfast area.

Several weeks later, a friend asked her to accompany her to an antique store. She went, and there was a china cabinet. If it was not the original one owned by her grandmother, it certainly was its twin. There was no difference. She was delighted until she heard the cost.

"That didn't deflate me, and I didn't entertain any doubt that I would have it," she assured me. "I told my husband about it, and he went to look at it. He agreed it certainly would be perfect for our breakfast area, but at this time, our budget would not handle it. We left the store, and on the way home, my husband carefully explained the many reasons why we could not afford it. I listened and said nothing. I can honestly tell you I did not mention the china cabinet again. I merely knew it was mine and visualized it standing against the bare wall."

"Two months later, when a delivery truck backed into our driveway, I thought they had the wrong house," she continued. "The man who rang the doorbell asked me where I wanted my china cabinet placed. Shortly after, when my husband arrived home, he found me in tears, stroking the beautiful carvings on my polished china cabinet. He also knew it was mine and found no problem paying for it. He told me that the day he chose to go back and look at it in the hopes he could get it at a reduced price, he found to his delight, that it had been marked down to half price. The store was in the process of moving to a new location and had reduced all of their merchandise for quick removal."

Some of you might be saying, "That's not so great. I always get what I'm after when I nag long enough." Another might think, "My, what an unusual husband she has. Mine would be too tight." Still, others may not even want an antique china cabinet.

The moral of this story: No naggin'; no negative thinking that the price made it unobtainable; just steady, positive energy, and a knowing it would be her china cabinet.

I have to admire this beautiful, positive attitude because she then told me she was working on another major goal that she would materialize soon.

What's your pleasure? Don't just sit there.

SELECT IT! PROJECT IT! EXPECT IT! COLLECT IT!

SPEC

SELECT – PROJECT
EXPECT – COLLECT

SPEC is the technique that I use when I have a goal to reach. It is not new; people from all walks of life use it in many cultures and professions. Follow me through the steps as I explain them in more detail.

Select a goal to get started. Someone asked me if this technique could be used for other purposes other than just entering contests for merchandise. YES! This can be used to obtain anything you desire in the physical, mental, or spiritual realms. You name it, and you can claim it.

Project it can be accomplished in many ways: See yourself as already having it. For example, the Natives see the rain falling on the ground while they are doing their famous Rain Dance. They do not see the beginning stages of clouds forming or darkening skies. Just the end result of rain hitting the ground. In the same way, a doctor, healer, or patient should always see the end result of the patient's perfect health.

That is, they must visualize the patient not getting well but instead already being 100% well. This is not lying to oneself; rather, this is commanding the Higher Consciousness to bring about a particular desired goal, condition, or situation into one's life.

Expect it is seeing yourself as already having or enjoying the end result. The following is a simple visualization technique I enjoy doing while waiting for something to come to fruition. It's a yoga breathing exercise that anyone can use. While sitting in a chair, inhale slowly for four to seven seconds or heartbeats (whichever is most comfortable for you); hold your breath for a four to seven beat count; exhale slowly for a four to seven beat count; finally, do not breathe at all for four to seven seconds. Repeat this breathing sequence for five minutes. While doing this rhythmic breathing, SEE yourself having what you want to have or being what you want to be.

NOTE: This technique is called Square Breathing. Breathe in for four, hold for four, exhale for four, hold for four, and repeat.

A certain phenomenon occurs as you do this special breathing exercise. As you slowly exhale about the fourth time, you will become aware of a very relaxed feeling in your arms and legs. You will feel so comfortable that you will not even want to move. This is because physical tension has been reduced within the muscles and nerves of your body.

At the same time, a second phenomenon occurs. Your anxieties and your mental tensions are also relieved. This leaves your thoughts and mind open for you to program your goals. In this relaxed state, mentally picture your desired end result.

Be positive! Ask for the good things of life. You deserve the best! How else can you express your God-given talents? How else can you help others unless you are healthy and happy? You need energy and a life of abundance to accomplish your best work. This technique has proven very successful for me and many of the students that use it.

Being a positive person is so vital and important to make this process and life, in general, a daring, delightful adventure. Beware, I'm going to do more preaching on the subject. First, is to think positive, do not be negative either mentally or emotionally. Do not dwell on what could go wrong or what has not worked before. This is a new moment! Visualize the end result only, and do not be concerned with how it will come to you. Just see and feel it as though it is already achieved. Second, do something constructive on the physical level to aid your mental picture. You have to 'get into the act.'

You can accomplish this by using the yoga exercise I shared with you earlier or by depriving yourself of some physical pleasure until you receive what you want.

For example, one woman kept the TV turned off for weeks until she received (from unexpected sources) the money she needed to repair her house.

Another student got on her treadmill and walked 15 minutes a day until she got a new car. She explained, "I visualized myself in a new car. I could actually smell the newness of the interior." She won the car from a local radio station contest three months later. You may use whatever disciplinary measure you wish that fits into your way of life. The important thing is that you do something to show your subconscious mind that you mean business, and that you are willing to work for what you want to invest the energy in order to manifest your desire.

In this way, you become positive by doing some extra tasks on the physical level. If you fail to do the exercise or to use the discipline you have chosen, this is an indication to the subconscious that you really did not want or care to accomplish what you asked for.

Yes! Sometimes I have collected a prize or end result in a matter of hours, but the majority of the time, there is a delayed result; that is when the majority of people get impatient and can actually nullify their goal with negative energy. Being positive in all areas is a way of life for me. Make it one for you.

Collect it is the fun part and makes it all worthwhile. The most important component of this is to begin to love completely. LOVE everything unconditionally: the clouds, wind, stones, trees, animals, insects, and all the people you come into contact with. (This is sometimes the most difficult task.) You must love and respect everything. This is not physical love but rather a universal feeling, a common bond, and harmony with all. My Native American friend taught me that even the stones have a consciousness of their own. God's consciousness is in everything, and we must love all of it!

I tend to get sentimental when I remember all the good things and experiences I've had and continue to enjoy. I have found that the more you use those techniques in all areas of your life, the more insightful you become. A calm, contented feeling will surface when you realize what life in the physical is all about. You will find yourself becoming more of an observer, and your understanding of people will take on a new perspective. It will also remind you that we are all here to learn about ourselves as we evolve. We are all 'Gods in the making' as the saying goes.

PART TWO

INTRODUCTION #2

The second part of this book is a step-by-step guide to entering contests to win as a fun and profitable hobby. It provides technical know-how and specific action to take toward acquiring your goals. It lists how to set up your contest files and keep records.

The portions of my daily diary of personal experiences will be shared honestly and accurately and should prove to be most helpful and simple to understand.

I will make no statement or guarantee that you will be a consistent winner. I can only share with you what I did and what results I accomplished. Is it worth the time and postage money for you? You must decide.

I still receive letters from people who read the first part of this book and have benefited from my suggestions. It is truly nice to hear from you and about your wins—more power to you.

"What have you won lately?" still seems to be the opening statement by many that write to me or by people I meet when I lecture.

To answer the main question, yes, we are still living in and enjoying the dream home we won some years ago.

Some new interests sparked for me after the house win: Power of the Mind, Self-hypnosis, Silva Mind Development, and 'Self-I-Wareness.'

I have studied all courses and programs, here and abroad, on these subjects. I wanted to understand 'me' better. During my active traveling and lecturing from coast to coast, I no longer had the time or interest to enter sweepstakes and creative writing contests.

One June, several years ago, Pat, my husband, retired from his '8 to 5' job. I reached another decision. To stay home and write full time. I'd met so many exciting and interesting people during my lecturing and travels; I wanted to write and teach others how they could solve their problems and projects with a positive attitude. I began typing and getting it on paper from the notes I'd gathered.

I am still compiling the information. I also decided to once again contest for the fun of it.

I started sending entries that same month my husband retired, just to get back in the swing of it. I did not keep a record of my daily activities or how many entries I submitted. I did, however, keep a record of what I won from that June to December period. The following is what I won: a travel clock, toy, Schaeffer pen set, leather belt, billfold with $100 check, gold money clip, check for $1,000, canvas bag, $50 gift certificate plus a personalized coffee mug, theatre tickets, and dinner.

Beginning in January, I kept a daily calendar diary of my entries sent, postage, time I allotted, and items won.

I feel that anyone can relate to this at-a-glance record and perhaps may wish to use the guidelines for their contesting.

May you reap the rewards, pleasure, and success that I continue to find in this exciting hobby of entering contests to WIN.

Helene Hadsell

KEYS TO WINNING

How many of you have visions of opening a letter one day and finding a check for $100,000, a phone call telling you that you just won in the Readers Digest promotional sweepstakes, the Publisher's Clearing House sweepstakes, or any of the other sweepstakes that are going on today? Somebody wins; why not you? Are they just lucky? Do they know the judging agency, the director, or the sponsor? What is the catch, the secret of being a consistent winner?

Winning big in sweepstakes, creative writing contests, or lotteries may be fantasies to some, but to more and more people, these dreams are becoming a reality. In the past, it was women who entered contests and won the most prizes. Housebound with small children, limited in experience or education, she dreamed of all the extras that could be obtained by entering contests. She won because her desire was so intense, and she mentally made it happen. 'WISHING WILL MAKE IT SO' is not fiction; it's fact.

NOTE: I believe Helene is referring to Evelyn Ryan, the protagonist in the book The Prize Winner of Defiance Ohio. A must-read for anyone who loves this hobby.

Today, more and more men's names are appearing on winner's lists, and they are capturing some of the big prizes, especially in recipe contests. In a local recipe contest recently sponsored by a newspaper, twenty prizes were offered. The four top winners were men, the ladies only captured eight of the prizes, and the rest of the prizes were awarded to men.

At the present time, our area supermarkets are distributing Bingo tickets with each store visit.

"The men are making more trips to purchase one item to get the tickets than women are," said several grocery checkers when I asked what the response was.

So what does that tell us? Why, that just about everyone likes the idea of taking a chance, buying a ticket, and sending in their entry to a sweepstakes contest so they can be declared a WINNER!

95

WHY NOT?

Anyone can get on the BRAND WAGON and cook with an AMANA RADARANGE, sew on a SINGER, fly via UNITED or AMERICAN to that special place. I call it the NAME IT AND CLAIM IT GAME because that is exactly what I have been doing, off and on, for the past twenty years.

Whether it's lotteries, bingo tickets, mailing entries, checking numbers, or registering for door prizes, it's FUN and EXCITING being a WINNER.

Unfortunately, not everyone wins. If you have ever kept a track record of winners, be it in sports, art, literature, acting, and yes, even in contesting, you will find that most of the people win consistently. The same names appear on top of the winner's list. What is their secret?

I've read enough of their comments and listened to their interviews to realize there is a common denominator with winners:

- They decide what they want.
- They imagine they have it.
- They KNOW they will get it.

HOW THE RIGHT ATTITUDE MAKES A WINNER

Deciding what you want, imagining you have it, and KNOWING it will be yours are the KEYS to being a winner. There is one more attribute that is obvious with most of the winners: their attitude.

"You are what you think." I'm sure you are all familiar with that phrase. In the past (now just stop and think for a minute), did you have good luck? Get the job you wanted? Did you ever win anything in a raffle, at Bingo, or at the races? Was it consistent, or are you a BORN LOSER? Nothing ever went right. Somebody else always wins. Chances on lotteries or postage spent on sweepstakes were a waste of time and money.

Now give it some thought. How was your attitude? The idea seemed like a good one at the time. I wanted to win because heaven knows I could use the money.

Did you harbor guilty feelings about winning? Many times this comes from our religious background: *"I shouldn't ask for material things. That's a sin."*

YOU ARE WHAT YOU THINK, remember. It shouldn't take you too long to now realize that what you thought in the past, you actually are now.

"Okay, I'll buy that," you may now agree. "So, how do I go about changing my thinking, my attitude, and my luck to become a winner?" The answer is: THINK IT, DO IT, BELIEVE IT.

The first step is so simple you may overlook it until you discipline yourself to become aware of what you think. Although this book is slanted toward being a winner in contests, you and I both know that LIFE IS A GAME. We can play the game to be a winner.

When you apply the following principles, they will carry over to all facets of your life, your job, marriage, health, and wealth.

Begin today to become aware of your thinking. In the past, if you thought, *"Not me,"* change it to, *"Why not me?"* Change the phrase *"I can't"* to *"I can."*

Today is a new day and a new beginning. Anything you thought or spoke about in the past that meant doubt, failure, or was of a negative nature is gone and buried. You need no longer dwell in the past, nor need to identify with any hardship, heartache, or heartbreak you experienced. Realize you are a POWERFUL person.

Every thought you harbor in fear, anger, or pain seems to accumulate more energy, and it will eventually become a reality. *"Hang in there long enough and strong enough, and you will get it,"* is a cosmic law. *'There are no failures, only delays in results'* also applies here. How long it takes to manifest depends on the energy and thought directed to it.

Would it not make sense for you to achieve a healthy, wealthy, successful winner's attitude in all areas? You MUST now think in a constructive, positive way.

I AM A WINNER, and I WILL ACHIEVE ALL MY GOALS.

NOTE: Do not shame or berate yourself if your goals do not manifest. Shame is insidious. We don't even know we are doing it to ourselves.

Remember, even Helene gave up after two years and bought the color TV. Her goal did manifest. Helene got her TV. She just didn't win it.

The key is to release your attachment to the outcome. As Colette Baron Ried teaches, always ask when co-creating and manifesting, "This or something better, for the highest good of all."

WHAT DO YOU WANT?

What do you wish to achieve? What is your desire? Let's find out and get on with living, loving, and learning in the classroom of life, where the MEEK shall inherit the earth only if they have the DESIRE.

ACQUIRE A DESIRE TO WIN WHAT?

You already have a desire to be a winner, or you wouldn't be reading this book. But what is it you want to win in the contest game? Is it a new car, a trip, money, a home, a boat, or a skateboard? What, exactly???

Some of the following suggestions were given by students that attended my classes (not necessarily available from contests).

BETTER JOB ... BETTER LIFE
LOTS OF MONEY ... SEXY WIFE

FOREIGN CAR ... PRIVATE PLANE
NAME IN LIGHTS ... CLAIM TO FAME

ROCKING CHAIR ... COLOR TV
PLACE IN COUNTRY ... SECURITY

I WANT TO WIN THE FOOTBALL POOL,
AND THEN SIT BACK WHILE OTHERS DROOL

WHO ME?   ALL I WANT IS
PEACE-POWER-PERFECTION

MAKE MINE...
KNOWLEDGE ... WISDOM ... UNDERSTANDING

What does the five-year-old neighbor girl want? Why all she wants is a handful of bubble gum—NOW. She wants to make the bubble as big as her friend, Cindy. One that will cover her entire face. (It so happened I had a pound package of bubble gum on hand. I'm a bubble blower, too.) She had her desire immediately.

Some of our desires may take a bit longer to set into motion. Bear in mind; THERE ARE NEVER ANY FAILURES, ONLY DELAYS IN RESULTS.

Once, on New Year's Day, I made a list of things I wanted to win in the sweepstakes and contest games of that coming year.

1. A microwave oven. I have one I use daily in my kitchen. I found it to be so handy and time-saving; I also wanted one for our lake cabin.

2. A new car. A gas saver. I had never won a car, and I thought it would be a good project at which to aim. I even got specific and made it white with blue upholstery.

3. A trip to Hawaii. No, I've never been to Hawaii. Sure, I've been to Europe six times, even to Russia and the interior of Mexico several times, but not Hawaii, not yet!

4. Any other wins, I wanted cash. That's a BIG ORDER, you may think. I look at it as being a lot of fun. How long will it take to accomplish these goals? When I have projected enough energy to make them reality, and I have visualized having them until I have accomplished my goals. There is no set time.

Perhaps you may want to start with one item. Okay, it's your show, so get in the act.

I feel the more one thinks and visualizes his goals and desires, the more energy is directed to the project, and the sooner it can be accomplished. In order to make it a daily reminder, I took a 5" x 7" blank card, and with a marks-a-lot, I printed in bold letters, MICROWAVE OVEN. CAR. HAWAII. MONEY.

I taped it to the dash of my little Hornet I drove and planned to replace. I taped another card, saying the same thing on the bookrack that sits on my desk. This simply reminded me to give my projects energy by thinking about them. Every time I read the cards, I briefly closed my eyes (it only takes twenty to thirty seconds) and saw the microwave oven sitting in the corner of my kitchen counter at our lake cabin. This was just imagining that I had it there already.

I had my husband measure the space it required and asked him to extend the counter to accommodate the oven so it would be ready when I won it. He did it one morning. He even found the same counter material that matched the existing counter, and we were ready.

My husband is my greatest *WINspiration*. He not only encourages me in all my ventures, but he projects the end-result image for me, too.

It was January 1st when I began to project for a microwave oven. It was February 22nd when I received the phone call from the local representative of the Rath Meat Company. He told me I had won an Amana Radarange for the winning recipe I submitted in their recipe contest.

I scratched MICROWAVE OVEN off my list and began concentrating on the car, Hawaii, and money prizes.

My car end result picture was me sitting behind the wheel of a white car with blue upholstery. My imagination got so vivid; I was beginning to smell the newness of the interior. When I thought of my trip to Hawaii, I pictured my husband and me walking on the beach. We both had on bathing suits, and it was warm and sunny.

THE DIFFERENCE BETWEEN DESIRE & KNOWING

It was Sunday, March 27th, when I spotted the full-page ad in the Dallas paper announcing that a local radio station, KLIF, and the local area Datsun dealers were giving away twelve Datsuns, two a week for the next six weeks. Ah-ha, I thought, an opportunity to get my car.

Requirements were to register at a local dealer or mail in a card to the radio station. Rules stated there would be a drawing of all entries received.

The radio personality (D.J. to me) would make the calls and ask the question, "What is your favorite radio station?" Your answer to be a winner had to be "KLIF 1190 is my favorite radio station." A week after the close of the contest, the twelve winners would gather at a local showroom, and there would be a drawing of keys to find out which Datsun you won. Would it be a Hustler, an 8-210, an F-I Sports Wagon, or a Honeybee?

After reading the ad, I got so excited I didn't bother reading the rest of the paper at that time. I went to my desk immediately. The contest was to begin on Monday, which was the very next day, so I wanted to get some entries in on the first day because chances would be better with fewer entries. In a contest where drawings are held over a period of time, it's best to get in on the first of it, then continue to send in one or more entries each day until your name is called. By 2:00 PM Sunday, I had mailed four cards.

Copying a sample entry blank pictured in the ad, I used colored poster board and cut-out cards in the shape of the car pictured in the newspaper ad. The time spent doing it added positive energy to my goal. It takes a little effort on your part to set up the situation for yourself, but it's fun being creative.

I'd venture to say hundreds of thousands of people noticed the full-page ad, and I'm sure many found it interesting and had a desire to win one of the cars; some would put the ad aside to give it further study, and some would actually cut out the blank and mail it, which would be the first step. It takes one more step to be a winner: to picture yourself having the car or being in the car or whatever your creative imagination comes up with.

Monday morning began fun-and-game time for me, waiting for the call, making me a car winner. Fortunately, the station plays country and western music, and I really dig it. You didn't have to listen to the radio all day. You simply had to answer correctly when they called. In order not to goof when they called, perhaps forget to mention KLIF 1190, and lose out, I placed a card beside the phones throughout the house. Each one said, *"When a D.J. calls and asks you what your favorite radio station is, this is what you answer (exactly): 'KLIF 1190 is my favorite radio station.'"* This was also for my husband's use in case they called when I wasn't home.

About two o'clock on Monday, they announced the first winner, a girl in Dallas. One down, eleven to go. *"Which one will I be?"* I asked myself. On Friday, they called a man in Fort Worth, and he gave the correct answer. In the meantime, I mailed in one entry each day. I also made a trip to the Datsun dealer and looked at the cars. I also signed up and put my name in their hopper.

The following week I listened whenever I was at home. I realized that they called people on Monday and Friday. Monday, they announced another winner. That left nine cars.

It was Friday, April 8th, when I woke up and KNEW I would win a car that day.

At this point, let me define the difference between DESIRE and KNOWING. DESIRE IS EXCITED ANTICIPATION; KNOWING IS CALM ASSURANCE. For example, you are present at a drawing, and your first three numbers are called. You feel like you are about to explode. The last number is called, and you missed by one number.

This is a DESIRE feeling and very common. You have repressed energy, and you want it to happen. Unfortunately, there has not been enough energy projected to make it so at that time.

When you KNOW something, it is a different feeling. You have a calm, cool assurance; all anxiety is gone; it is already done. All that now remains is to experience the physical presentation BEING CALM AND COOL WHEN YOU COLLECT. It is a good feeling.

Become aware of this KNOWING feeling in all areas of your life, and you are well on your way to total 'I-wareness.'

It's not negative to KNOW you're not going to win at something sometimes. It just lets you KNOW that enough energy has not been projected to make it a reality.

You can play games and kid yourself by quitting your job because you have the DESIRE to win a $100,000 prize. Until you know the difference between DESIRE and KNOWING, don't be foolhardy. Keep your job. One day you will know the difference with 'I-wareness.'

Several years ago, I gave a lecture to a group of businesswomen at a convention in Fort Worth; the literature that was mailed out to the membership about my being the speaker must have impressed one of the women. She approached me just before the program began and told me her desire. Tomorrow night, the last night of the convention, they would have a drawing for a door prize. The prize was an ocean cruise. "I want it so badly I can taste the salt water," she said.

"My husband and I are having problems, and I feel if we have this time together, we can work it out," she continued. "I know if you project enough energy for me to win this cruise, I will get it," she concluded. She gave a sigh, and a calmness came over her.

"You already have the cruise," I assured her. "Tomorrow night, when they have the drawing, and they call your name, act surprised. They expect you to."

For a moment, she thought I was jesting, then she said with enthusiasm, "I'll call you and tell you."

Shortly after eight o'clock the following night, she called. "I won! I KNEW I would after I talked to you, but how did you know?" she asked. "Do you recall when you sighed as if a great burden had been lifted off your shoulders?" I asked.

"Why yes," she said, "I was so relieved that I got to talk to you before the program. I was concerned someone might get to you first and ask you to help them win," she explained.

As a matter of fact, someone else had approached me earlier and asked for my help to win. I did. She obviously didn't want this particular cruise. That's not to say she will never take or win a cruise. It only means that, at this time, there wasn't enough energy projected by her to make it happen. If it remains important to her, she should continue to give it energy until she is actually on the ship. The majority of people never complete their goals. They jump to something else.

A number of years ago, I had a dream, and it was a 'lulu.' I was in a great hall that was packed with merchandise. There were cars, boats, clothes, furniture, appliances, and TVs. A man was standing at the door as if waiting. I asked who all this merchandise belonged to. His answer was, *"This is the place where people's dreams are stored. The trouble is, they give up and release the energy too soon, so I keep them in storage. Once in a while, some of them get back to it and claim their dreams."*

Do any of you have something stored in that room? Don't be flighty. If you have a goal or desire, hang in there until you get it. Also, I must advise you to make sure you want it before you send out all that good energy.

Before concluding our conversation, I told the cruise winner that if her marriage was as important to her as the winning of that trip, I was certain that she could solve that problem, cruise or not.

Projecting energy toward any goal with steady determination will eventually be fruitful. This applies to any situation.

In contesting, it makes it doubly exciting when you get the KNOWING feeling because it means you have succeeded in your project, and it's time to make another goal. A wise man once said, "The three things in life that make it worthwhile are: to feel useful by doing something, to be loved by someone, and to have something to look forward to."

It was shortly after 4:00 PM on the day I KNEW I was going to win my car. The phone rang. It was my husband. He was fixing the plumbing at our rental house. He had broken a pipe and wanted me to go to the plumber for a fitting. I didn't want to go because I wanted to be home when the radio station called to tell me I was their fourth Datsun winner. I might call this 'the supreme test with self.' I was so sure I would win; I told myself they would only call after I got back home since it would take less than half an hour. I left. It was the Friday before Easter, and many of the shops closed early. I had to go from hardware to hardware store. I finally found the fitting and took it to my husband. When I got back home, it was after 6:00 PM. I turned on the radio, and the D.J. just announced that they now had four winners and would call the people again Monday. I couldn't believe it. How had I missed? I was so sure my KNOWING feeling was right.

The phone rang. It was my oldest son; he had an apartment on the other side of town and came over occasionally for a free meal or to check to see if he had any mail.

"Hey mom, I won a Datsun about an hour ago," he calmly announced. He had come by the house to check the mail when the phone rang. Someone asked to speak to me. He told them I wasn't there, but could he help or take a message? "Why yes, you can; what is your mother's favorite radio station?"

"For a second, I was taken off guard," he told me, "I then saw the card taped to the phone and knew what it was all about. So I answered, 'KLIF 1190 is her favorite radio station.'"

"Your mom will be proud of you tonight. You just won her a new Datsun," he announced.

Later I heard the taped call when they played back the conversation with my son. The big question: Would I have won that Friday had my son not been there to answer the phone? As I listened the week earlier, several times when they made calls and there was no answer, they drew another name. Was my son supposed to be there at that time to make it possible? I don't have the answer. I just KNEW I would win that day.

NOTE: Currently, most official rules state the entrant must be the one that qualifies or wins the prize. Therefore in this example, Helene would have been disqualified as it was her son who answered, regardless if he had the right answer or not. That said, if Helene were contesting now, she would have a cell phone with her.

When all twelve winners were drawn, we all gathered at the showroom to draw for our keys to one of the twelve cars. There was no white car with blue upholstery.

Instead, I won a blue pick-up truck. That certainly was not the car I had projected.

To me, that was not the end result. I put an ad in the paper the following week and sold it. This win turned out to be MONEY.

Sure, I could have gone out and bought a car, the one I wanted, with the money I received for selling the truck, but that's not the way I wanted it. There was still a white car with blue upholstery out there for me to WIN.

For the rest of that year, I won minor merchandise prizes and a number of cash prizes. Yes, enough to buy my car and take a trip to Hawaii. That wouldn't be any fun. I had the patience to continue to project energy until I got the phone call telling me of a Hawaii trip, a car, or big money prize wins.

Someone once said it takes patience, persistence, and postage to be a contest winner. I agree with that statement, but I believe the thing that makes it happen is the energy you direct toward it. Don't rely on LUCK. LUCK is like a rubber crutch: it will let you down when you try to lean on it.

MAKE IT HAPPEN. Decide what you want and help it along by giving it energy for your end result accomplishment.

Entering contests is an excellent avenue to pursue because it offers the material things you should have been accustomed to a long time ago.

SUPPLIES FOR THE CONTESTOR

In the contesting business, like any other, a penny saved is a penny earned. Supplies make up a large chunk of the cost and are, therefore, a target for economy.

NOTE: Helene was a sweeper/contestor in the 60s, 70s, and 80s. She did not enter online or on a cell phone. Please keep this in mind when reading the next several chapters, if you feel her advice is outdated. That said, her advice for mail-ins and tracking is still applicable.

ENVELOPES

1. Check both office supply and discount stores for sales.

2. The unit prices are significantly lower when you buy larger quantities at the same time.

3. If space for storing supplies is limited, you can share larger purchases with other contestors.

4. Don't overlook the economy of re-using envelopes you receive. If they haven't been marked up too badly, you might paste colorful tape or use a colored pencil to cover up the return address.

5. Call or visit the local print shops. Many times they are overstocked, or envelopes become misprinted and are rejected. You can get them at a low cost and cover up the printing with a stick-on-slogan, a marks-a-lot pen, or whatever.

6. Envelope size or color, in most instances, does not matter when entering sweepstakes. Many times contest rules state that only a #10 (9 1/2" x 4 1/8") or smaller size envelope can be submitted. **FOLLOW THE RULES TO THE LETTER.**

PENS AND PENCILS

Pens and pencils are cheaper in large quantities. Do keep a good supply of colored pens on hand. It's easier to write with them, and it breaks the monotony of using the same color.

PAPER AND CARDS

Most rules call for submitting your name on a 3" x 5" piece of paper. In that case, any type of paper is permissible. Again, I suggest you make friends with print shops. They sometimes have test copies and overruns they cannot use. Business offices often discard their old letterhead stationery or revised forms. Ask friends who work in offices, as that is a source from which you might benefit. Any color or weight of paper is fine.

Some rules state to print your name on a 3" x 5" card. If this is their request, then, by all means, use a card. The index cards can be purchased at any discount store. Perhaps you have an unclaimed freight store in your area. That, too, is a good source for less expensive paper products.

One of my contesting friends gets her paper from the newspaper printing dock. They usually have roll ends available that they discard. She has a paper cutter and always has a good supply of 3 x 5's on hand. She is also generous, and we all benefit from her supply. FREE IS MUCH BETTER THAN CHEAP.

KEEPING RECORD

I keep a detailed record of contest activities on a giant-sized calendar, a worthwhile investment. Each day, as I take my envelopes out of the file box, I count the stamps I stick on and make a note of how many I send. I also make a note of how much time I allotted to signing my name or addressing envelopes.

Write down every penny spent on paper, envelopes, and stamps. That is part of expenses and can be deducted at the end of the year for income tax records. Be sure to write a check or get a receipt from the post office for the stamps purchased. This is your biggest expense. Don't begrudge the postage money spent. When I stamp my envelopes before I mail them off, I mentally project positive energy to each envelope by thinking: *"HERE GOES ANOTHER WINNER THAT WILL BRING ME BACK MY END RESULT."*

Don't be like the woman I once had as a neighbor. One evening she called and asked if she could drive to the post office with me. (We talked earlier over the fence, and she knew I was going to make a trip later.) She entered contests half-heartedly because she knew I kept winning things. When we reached the Post Office, she leaned out to deposit our entries in the curb letterbox.

As she slipped them in the slot, she turned to me and said, "Well, there goes nothing." I was dumbfounded. She never did win anything while I knew her. Later she moved out of the neighborhood and took her gloom with her.

We all have 'down' periods occasionally. If it is a constant thing, it really is the pits. If this happens to you, make a considerable effort to get back into a positive frame of mind. Read something uplifting; listen to violin music—it is one of the most uplifting, soothing sounds one can experience. Remember, you are in control of your thinking. Change it if it's pulling you down.

THE STEPS I TAKE TO ENTER CONTESTS

The following is an example of a contest I had entered. Please note: The rules state entries must be postmarked by October 17th. For a postmark deadline of October 17th, I mailed in my last entry on the 13th or 14th of October to be safe.

SAFEGUARD'S SMALLEST SWEEPSTAKES. GRAND PRIZE: (1) 2-week trip for two to the smallest countries in Europe—Monaco, The Vatican, Liechtenstein, Luxembourg, etc. worth $5,000, or a cash alternative of $5,000. FIRST PRIZE: (5) Sony Color TVs. SECOND PRIZE: (10) Litton Microwave Ovens. THIRD PRIZE: (20) Polaroid SX-70 Cameras. FOURTH PRIZE: (1000) Novus Calculators. OPEN TO: U.S. residents, including residents of Florida. VOID: Missouri, Ohio, Utah, Vermont, and wherever prohibited by law. DEADLINE: Entries must be postmarked by October 17, 1977. HOW TO ENTER: On an Official Entry Form or 3" x 5" plain piece of paper, handprint your name, address, zip code, and phone number. Each entry submitted must be accompanied by either of the following: two (2) wrappers from any size of Safeguard, or a 3" x 5" plain piece of paper on which you have printed the words "Safeguard's Smallest Soapstakes." Enter as often as you wish but mail each entry separately in a hand-addressed envelope no larger than 9 1/2" x 4 1/8" (#10 envelope) to: Safeguard's Smallest Soapstakes, P.O. Box 1831, Blair, Nebraska 68009. Sweepstakes participation via entry blanks distributed in retail stores is void in Wisconsin, Maryland, West Virginia, and South Dakota.

Contest promotions usually advertise three to five months before their deadline dates. Why get in a dither and frustrated when you can address and prepare your entries using the following method:

1. After reading the Rules, decide how many you want to send.

2. Get your envelopes from your stored supply and address one envelope this way: wherever I intend to paste the stamp, I write the date I want to start mailing and when I want to mail my last entry.

3. Next, count out 100 3" x 5" pieces of paper and, with a rubber band, secure them with the fifty envelopes. Fifty pieces of paper are for printing your name, address, zip code, and telephone number. The other fifty are for printing the words: 'Safeguard's Smallest Soapstakes.' When you have free time, you can address your envelopes. Be sure to handprint the envelopes as the rules indicated.

When I watch TV, sit under the dryer at the beauty parlor, or in the car on the way to our lake cabin with my husband, I usually have two or three packets ready to be addressed. It's really an easy, simple way to enter contests when you follow a system. When I am finished with my addressing, it only takes a few minutes to file them. I use this procedure in all the contests I enter.

NOTE: If Helene were entering now, she would be using her downtime to send in text sweeps or enter social media contests on her cell phone, organizing them on her browser or using RoboForm.

If I find entry blanks in grocery stores or drug stores, I use them. Magazines many times carry contest rules. I have found from experience that whether you use an official entry blank or a 3" x 5" piece of paper or card makes absolutely no difference in your chances of winning. The main thing is to enter. Whether you send in two, twenty, or two hundred, try to enter every contest that comes along; that is, if you're interested in the prizes offered.

WHEN TO MAIL

Some people like to mail their entries all at once at the beginning, middle, or end of the contest. Judging firms claim that over half of the entries submitted in contests come in the last two weeks before the deadline.

This is the method I use for mailing entries: after I address the envelopes, I space them in my file box at several different times before the last mailing date. In the Safeguard contest, the closing date was October 17th. I had my fifty envelopes addressed on

September 18th. I spaced them between September 18th and the postmarked date of October 17th. Some days I mailed two, some days one, and some days more. I use this method because I like to have a chance of getting in on more than one mailbag.

Let me explain what I mean by that.

In my research and reading on how sweepstakes are selected, I became aware of the following information: On the day a sweepstakes drawing is held by the judging agency, the canvas mail sacks, full of entries, are numbered. If there are fifty sacks, then fifty slips of paper are placed in a metal selection drum, numbered 1 to 50. Each numbered slip of paper represents a corresponding numbered mail sack.

To select the grand prize winner, an executive from the judging firm is blindfolded and led to the selection drum. The drum is rotated several times to ensure random selection. The executive reaches through the hinged opening at the top of the drum and retrieves a single piece of paper. The number is read, and still blindfolded, the person doing the drawing is led to the mail sack with the corresponding number. They reach in and pull out one envelope. The selection of entries is continued in this manner until all winners of the contest are drawn.

Postmark is checked to ensure compliance with the closing date. Five out of every hundred entries selected as winners are disqualified. Why? Using the incorrect size of 3" x 5" paper; using a rubber stamp to indicate the name and address when the rules require the entrant to 'print' that information; writing in script-style instead of printing; entries postmarked after closing date; failure to indicate on the entry form the name and address of the store where entry blank was obtained or where you shop. This question is often asked, and the answer just had to be included.

The majority of winners use a 3" x 5" piece of paper instead of an official entry blank. Only a small number of winning entries contain a box top or wrapper. Most winners use a substitute of a 3" x 5" to print the product name.

NOTE: You can use a similar method for single-entry online sweepstakes. You can bookmark the giveaway page to enter mid-entry period for a similar effect of being in the middle of the entry pool for the computerized random drawing programs.

GETTING AN AFFIDAVIT

When you win a contest and receive written notification from the judging firm or sponsor, sometimes you are required to sign a form to verify your name, address, and Social Security Number. You are asked to have it notarized and then return it in the self-addressed envelope they provide you. Be sure to make a copy for yourself. If you don't receive a prize or hear from the company in a reasonable length of time, you will know where to write.

NOTE: If you wish to learn how to find, organize, enter and win sweepstakes and giveaways, you can master the art of contesting, step-by-step in my book How To Win Cash, Cars, Trips & More! Combine that with Helene's SPEC method, and you have a modern winning formula.

WHEN TO PROJECT AND GIVE ENERGY

When you do the writing and addressing of the envelopes for a certain contest, paint a mental picture of the prize you want to win. When you mail the envelope, give it energy that it will be the winner. Whenever it comes to mind, and it will again, see yourself as already having and enjoying the prize.

LOOK FOR EXCITING THINGS TO HAPPEN,
BECAUSE THEY WILL!

THE QUESTIONS MOST OFTEN ASKED BY STUDENTS

1. What about income tax?

Contest winnings, with expenses deducted, are treated as ordinary income. Don't begrudge paying your taxes. Seventy-five percent of something is better than one hundred percent of nothing. Consult your IRS for specific cases.

2. When will they let me know I won?

After the winners are selected by the judging firm, the sponsor prints a list of the winners. They will mail you a copy if you request it, as long as you include a self-addressed stamped envelope.

It may be a week or two after the contest is judged before you are notified. You may get a phone call (if it is a large prize), or you may get a letter telling you of your win. If you've won one of the smaller prizes, you simply get the package of whatever it is and a note saying this is your prize for entering their contest. I have received packages three months after the close of a contest. Send for the winner's list if you want to make certain you did or did not win a particular contest.

3. Is it necessary to use a return address on my mailing envelope?

No, this is not necessary. If you do not use one, you may print, write, or use a rubber stamp or sticker. If you're sending in lots of entries, you'll find it time-consuming to use it. Do be sure the address you're sending is correct.

4. May I abbreviate the mailing address to save time?

Yes. Be careful what you abbreviate, though. You may abbreviate the 'Post Office Box' to simply 'Box,' and you may also abbreviate the state name. If you are sending thirty entries to Massachusetts, you'll save lots of time by simply using MA.

5. Does it help to use colored envelopes when entering sweepstakes?

No. The drawings are made by someone who is blindfolded. Therefore, any special colors, decorations, etc., are of no real advantage. Colored envelopes are also more expensive than plain white ones. I will say that if you BELIEVE colored envelopes will help you win, then you are directing more energy toward your win. Then it is your BELIEF (positive thinking) that is helping make it happen, rather than the color.

6. What is the difference between hand-printing, writing, and block letters?

'Write' means to write in cursive, as you would sign your name. 'Handprint' means you must print the required information by hand, not using a typewriter, stamp, or computer. If the rules say you must 'print' or 'handprint' in block letters, this means you must use ALL CAPITAL LETTERS. They don't have to be a work of art, just legible.

7. What is considered to be a plain piece of paper? Does the color matter? Is a card acceptable?

The color of paper you use makes no difference unless the rules call for a certain color (which is rare). A 'plain piece of paper' is simply that—a plain piece of paper.

No lines. No decorations. Again, color makes no difference unless specified. If the rules request a 'piece of paper,' then it may have lines, etc.

Usually, the rules will specify your paper to be a certain size (3" x 5" is the most common). In this case, be sure your paper is 3" x 5", not 3 1/4" x 5". Judging firms are sticklers on rules. Some even measure to see if the paper or card is 3" x 5". I understand they may allow 1/8" difference.

Some judges will accept a card in place of a piece of paper. But be safe rather than sorry. When the rules request paper, use paper. If they request a card, then use a card. You can always feel safe when you follow the rules EXACTLY!

8. What is the best-sized envelope to use?

The #10 (9 1/2" x 4 1/8") is probably best. It gives you the largest size without running the risk of being rejected. Some people will use very large manila envelopes. Naturally, this gives these entries an advantage. I'm sure this is the reason more and more rules are specifying an envelope *'no larger than 9 1/2" x 4 1/8" (#10 envelope).'* You may, of course, use smaller envelopes. There isn't much price difference per envelope between a #10 and a #6 3/4.

9. Is it necessary to print the quotation marks around the words to be printed?

Let's use an example: The rules say to print the words "Safeguard's Smallest Soapstakes" on a 3" x 5" piece of paper. Here the quote marks are used to set aside the words to be printed from the rest of the words in the sentence. You may or may not want to use these quotation marks in this instance. In another case, the rules may say to print the words: Dove's "Beautiful You" Sweepstakes. In this case, I would definitely use them since they are within a phrase to be printed.

10. Are the Second Chance Sweepstakes worth entering—or are most prizes awarded to Instant Winners?

Few, if any, prizes are usually won in 'Instant Winner' portions of sweepstakes. This means there are still many prizes to be awarded in the Second Chance Sweepstakes, which makes it worth entering.

NOTE: This advice has changed considerably, as many online sweepstakes have both grand prizes and instant prizes. Read the official rules for the prize and drawing details so you know how and when you can win.

11. Can I send entries in someone else's name?

Yes, but be sure they meet all the qualifications of the sweepstakes. The state in which they live must not be a 'void' state, and they must meet all other personal requirements that may be in the rules, such as age, licensed driver, etc. Keep in mind that if their name is drawn as a winner, the prize is awarded in their name, it must be reported on their income tax, and they may also have to pay taxes on the prize. All these things should be considered before you proceed.

12. What does it mean when the rules say that prizes are non-transferable?

It simply means the prize is awarded in the name of and to the person whose name is drawn as a winner. It will not be awarded in another person's name, even if requested. After the prize has been awarded, the winner may do whatever he or she wishes: keep it, sell it, or give it away.

13. How do you decide how many entries you want to mail into a particular contest?

I look at the prize list. If something excites me, like a trip to Hawaii, I send fifty entries.

Someone suggested this method of deciding how many entries to submit in each sweepstakes: Don't spend any more in postage than the value of the last prize. It's a rule of thumb but not always applicable.

You may find it helpful to set up a sweepstakes budget, allowing so much per month for postage. For example, you allow $25 per month. This means you can send in one hundred entries per month, which is about three entries a day. The consistent winners enter often and consistently.

NOTE: Firstly, as most entries are online now, your mail-in budget will not be calculated the same way Helene budgeted hers. Secondly, postage rates are not the same as they were when this book was originally written; therefore, your calculations for mail-in giveaways will have to be adjusted accordingly.

14. Which contests/sweepstakes should I send my entries to since there are so many?

First, the prizes should be prizes you would like to win. So, set yourself some prize goals like my family and I always have, then concentrate your entries on the contests and sweepstakes offering those prizes.

15. Do entries with the Official Entry Blank and proof-of-purchase stand a better chance of winning than those using a 3" x 5" substitute?

NO! It's just like colored envelopes. Drawings are made blindfolded and at random. In fact, most winners use the substitutes since the official entry blanks can be hard to find in large quantities. The same goes for the proof-of-purchase and its substitute. When entering sweepstakes, you are not required to make a purchase. When a sweepstakes asks for a proof-of-purchase (box top, end flap, wrapper, etc.), you will always find a substitute qualifier (hand-drawn facsimile) allowed. This is usually a 3" x 5" card with certain information required to be printed or written.

16. Are my chances of winning better in local contests and sweepstakes?

Definitely. Competition is less since entries are restricted to fewer people, in comparison with the national ones. Your local radio, TV, and newspaper should be paid attention to for these promotions. Use the same principles in these as you do in the national ones.

17. How many contests can you recall winning?

All of them. Life is a contest, and I consider myself a WINNER. Be it merchandise, a job, a health problem, or whatever. I certainly will not give up until I accomplish what I set out to do. To me, there are no failures, only a delay in results. When I accomplish one of my projects, I go on to another.

18. I just finished reading a book on a positive-principle outlook. It stated, '*Pray for what you will, but be willing to take what God gives you.*' What do you think of that suggestion? As a child, I was told it's the will of God for some people to be poor, and supposedly we were one of those 'unfortunate' families. I did not believe what I was being told, so I was on a search to find out what the real 'truth' was. (This is a direct quote from a letter I received.)

The book you read and quoted was the opinion of the author. My book is my opinion from my experiences to date. You, too, have an opinion and free will, and inwardly you know what is good for you. If your parents accepted poverty because they felt it was God's will, then that was their opinion and the limitation they placed on themselves. Whenever we reach the point of no return and say to ourselves, *"There has to be something more,"* we begin to make progress. Each day is a new day, a new beginning. We should never dwell in the past, except to realize what a fantastic learning experience we grew from.

I, too, was raised amid poverty, limitation, and religious dogma that kept me in bondage with guilt. I could not accept it, so I ventured out of the environment to do my own thing. I no longer accept or reject people or their opinions. I understand them. A number of years ago, I was given a copy of someone's concepts titled; *Desiderata.* I found so much encouragement, truth, and good sense in the writing, I keep a copy above my desk in my office lest I forget what this life is all about.

NOTE: I have included a copy of the poem Desiderata at the end of this book. I hope you find it as inspirational as Helene did.

19. Would you answer if I wrote you a letter to ask you something?

It depends on the letter. Many times it is not necessary. Someone may just write to tell me they won a trip after reading the book and they are getting a new outlook on life. Some have health problems and ask for energy to help them face or heal a situation.

If you have a number of questions and it warrants a reply, just send a self-addressed, stamped envelope, for I usually answer by return mail. I don't mind doing this because we are here to help each other.

NOTE: Like Helene, I frequently hear from 'sweepers.' Some people have won a prize and want to share the joy. Some send me their questions. I also answer those questions online (via blog, newsletter, video, social media post, etc.). If you have a question or comment, send it to me at questions@contestqueen.com

20. Does ESP have anything to do with contest-winning? How does one develop it?

Extra Sensory Perception or Effective Sensory Projection does help. The majority of people still think ESP means Extra Sensory

Perception, that few people have it, and you have ESP only if you can tell how many pennies someone has in his pocket.

Effective Sensory Projection is nothing but projecting energy toward an end result. Seeing it as already having it. Now anyone can do that. Effective Sensory Perception is just being aware of people and things around you. You can read people simply by listening to them and watching their body mannerisms.

If you are interested or have the desire to cultivate your ESP power, then do it. The more observant you become, the more you will come to realize that there is really nothing hidden. It's just that you never noticed it before.

21. To what do you attribute your luck, or is it luck?

Yes, there is LUCK, but you make your own luck with a positive attitude. One of the contest judges that met a number of top winners had this to say: "The big winners that I met and talked to all seem to have a positive attitude in all areas of their life." If you want to be lucky and have not been in the past, change your thinking, and your luck will follow.

22. Is the pursuit of material things selfish?

To some people, yes, if they think it is. For me, no. My concept of a selfish person is one that continues to want and accumulate things for the sheer joy of hoarding. When a person does not share, nor does he wish for anyone else to win or benefit from information, that person is selfish. To have creature comforts, good health, and happiness is everyone's birthright—claim it.

23. Can winning lead to happiness when you know so many lose?

Everyone has the same opportunity to find their place in the FUN if it's important enough to them. They can wallow in self-pity, be a BORN LOSER, but who keeps them there? They do. Of course, being a winner is fun. It's not a 'thing' that brings happiness; it's the person's attitude that determines that. Who was it that once said, "I would rather be rich and unhappy than poor and unhappy?" Think about it.

24. Why do different sweepstakes have different Post Office Boxes?

This is a way the sponsors key their sweepstakes advertising to measure responses from different parts of the country. It is a good idea to send your entries to different Post Offices when you have this information. As I said earlier, it will help get your entries into different mail sacks for the drawing.

25. Can I win more than one prize in a contest or sweepstakes?

Usually not. The rules will usually specify *"...only one prize per person (or household)."* This means no matter how many entries you sent or how many times your name was drawn, you can only win one prize.

26. Can I send more than one entry in an envelope in order to cut down on my postage?

Never—unless stated otherwise—and I've never seen it. Entries should always be mailed in separate envelopes unless the rules state otherwise.

27. When using a 3" x 5" paper or card for my name and address (instead of the official entry blank), can I print the other required information on the same 3" x 5" card?

Unless the rules state to print all required information on one 3" x 5" piece of paper, use two pieces. One as a substitute for the official entry blank and the other for your qualifier or proof-of-purchase substitute.

28. When the rules state that you must use an official entry blank, and I can't find any, how can I obtain them?

The best thing to do is to write to the sponsoring company with attention to the Advertising Department. Explain that you would like to enter their contest or sweepstakes but cannot find the blanks locally. Ask for them to send a few, and be sure to enclose a self-addressed, stamped envelope. Allow several weeks for their reply.

29. I noticed on some entry blanks there is a space for my phone number, but the official rules make no mention of having

to print this if using a 3" x 5" substitute. Should I include it anyway?

If the official rules do not specify the need for your phone number, then it is not necessary, even though the official entry blank has space for one. Feel safe by following those printed official rules.

30. How can I find out about all the contests and sweepstakes around the country?

Subscribe to a contest bulletin. I subscribe to several.

NOTE: You can find a list of sweepstakes aggregates that share legitimate giveaways on www.ContestQueen.com.

31. Do I have to send for a winner's list in order to find out if I've won and to claim my prize?

No. The company will contact you if you have won a prize. You may wish to send for a winner's list for those contests and sweepstakes that you enter, just to be sure.

32. Where is the 'Universal Product Code (UPC)' number requested in some sweepstakes?

It is the number appearing under the vertical bars on product packages.

33. How do I know contests and sweepstakes are legal?

They are closely monitored by the Federal Trade Commission. When drawings are held, a representative from the FTC or the US Postal Commission is present for observation. You can be assured the prizes will be awarded since a company would not spend a small fortune on sweepstakes advertising and then lose their reputation by not following through.

PART THREE

INTRODUCTION #3

Life is either a daring adventure or nothing.
Helen Keller

The publication of this book was an adventure for me. I had to crawl way out on the end of a long limb and self-publish the first edition, not knowing what the results might be. Looking back at that decision, I can see how much it changed my whole life. I've met fascinating people, traveled all over the world, and now enjoy teaching at my own center in Alvarado, Texas.

Some of the exciting highlights that come to mind are: in 1973, I was invited to Prague to present a paper on some ideas I have on apparitions and thought forms. I had DEJA'VU while in a palace in Moscow. Also, while in the Roman catacombs, I had a hairy and scary experience 'reviewing' my tomb.

On November 12th, 1986, I left for Peru to do some lecturing and workshops. I planned on a ten-day stay. I was there until January 20th of 1987. It would take a book to share my experiences during my stay there. Later, in July, I spent three weeks in Sedona, Arizona, to find out for myself about the rumors of the energy vortices. I am going to reserve my opinion on that experience for a future date. Perhaps I have a vivid imagination, but life is real for me. Someone remarked recently that SHIRLEY MACLAINE BETTER MOVE OVER ... because Helene Hadsell is a COSMIC ROVER, too.

I feel so fortunate to be on planet Earth at this time, with the stepping up of awareness and the untapped power of our collective minds that are waiting to be rediscovered. All my days and experiences are rewarding, uplifting, and exciting.

May yours also be.

Helene Hadsell

Be a Winner in All Areas of Your Life

Some of you reading this book may have read material of a similar nature. Perhaps you have been interested in entering contests and sweepstakes as a hobby, but somehow there were other projects that came first. You may be toying with the idea of getting serious and making the time for contesting on a regular basis. Don't be discouraged. Sometimes new ideas have to be presented a number of times before they are adapted.

I must share an interesting observation from one of my friends, Dr. Joseph Murphy, who wrote over forty-three books on the power of the mind. While lecturing in the Dallas area, he came to my home on several occasions. Because he was a down-to-earth person, I felt free to voice my opinions on his books and subject matter.

One day I commented. "Murphy, I find your books easy to read and understand, but I notice you say the same thing over and over again. In some of your books, you even repeat the same examples verbatim."

With a grin and twinkle in his steel-blue eyes, he replied, "Well, Helene, I figure if some people read something forty-two times, they may finally get it." Many times, repetition is the only way learning can be accomplished for some.

Recently, I received a letter from a young mother in Kansas. She started out by telling how she enjoyed reading THE NAME IT AND CLAIM IT GAME. She entered a few contests and intended to make it a rewarding hobby. That was three years ago. Personal family problems became so challenging she let it go by the wayside. Several months ago, after a divorce and a move, as she was sorting out her belongings, she rediscovered my book as she was unpacking boxes.

She stopped to reread some pages and became aware of something she had not noticed before.

"It was like reading a different book," she explained. "I realized what an upbeat sense of humor and attitude you have in all areas. NO FAILURES, ONLY A DELAY IN RESULTS stood out, and I now have borrowed that phrase for my temporary holdups. Sure, I want to win cars, trips, and money, and I will, but I KNOW what you were talking about when you said that we are all winners, but some of us have not realized it yet."

She continued, "It's only been a couple of months since I read the book for the second time. I now continue to review it and find new ideas. I borrowed some of your 'gems of wisdom,' as you call them, and I find myself repeating them daily. 'THOUGHTS BECOME THINGS ... CONCEIVE IT ... BELIEVE IT ... ACHIEVE IT'. This is one I really like: 'LIFE IS EITHER A DARING ADVENTURE OR NOTHING,' and 'PREPARE·FOR YOUR GOOD,' and 'WHAT GOD HAS DONE FOR OTHERS, HE NOW DOES FOR ME AND MORE.'"

"The phrases I mentioned above are tacked around our apartment for me and my two sons, ages nine and eleven, to read. I know my attitude has changed, and my sons are cultivating more confidence and a better attitude, also."

"Last Saturday, my nine-year-old son's name was drawn at the grocery store where we shop. He won a $50 merchandise certificate. He is having great fun planning how he will spend it. Monday, my eleven-year-old heard his name on the radio after sending in a postcard. He won dinner for two and a collection of records. Now it's my turn."

"My writing to you today has a two-fold purpose. First, to thank you for the super book you have written, and also to ask if you have more ideas about ways one can stay positive, constructive, and creative. I feel I've not been the best model in the past with my 'martyr' attitude. You notice I said the PAST. I assure you, that is where it will remain," she concluded.

It's letters like these that make my day.

Over my years of counseling people with all sorts of projects, I have compiled some ideas and techniques one can apply to suit one's particular needs. I feel we all have the power to create our own destinies and that we can help ourselves along the way by constructive thinking and actions. Why not tune into our creative forces and make this a more positive environment for ourselves and for those around us?

The more you are aware of your thoughts, and the more positive you are, the stronger and more powerful you become.

Also, you will find your positive end results happening faster. The two most important things before beginning any venture are: to KNOW what you want ... and to STAY with it until it is realized. When the thought comes to your mind, picture yourself as already having it.

HOW TO DEVELOP PICTURE POWER

If you have difficulty picturing a goal by imagining it, then cut out pictures to depict what it is you want. Paste the pictures on a piece of cardboard. Tack the pictures up on the wall or door, wherever you will see them often. Every time you look at the pictures, pretend you already have what you want. This way, you are giving your goals energy. Continue your imaging until your goal is realized.

NOTE: The reason this technique works is the subconscious works with images and pictures, not words. It's why vision boards can be a powerful manifesting tool.

SNAPPING FROM NEGATIVE TO POSITIVE THINKING

Wear a rubber band around your wrist and snap it every time you think or say something negative. Your negativity might manifest as follows: You may be irritable, dislike being around somebody, or get impatient. You may dwell on a physical problem and exaggerate it.

You may feel depressed, entertain unfounded fears, feel lonely, unworthy, or 'poor me, nobody likes or understands me.' Every time your thinking becomes negative, snap the rubber band and change your thinking. You already know what most of your DOWNERS are; why not make a list of some of the positives?

I TRUST MY GOOD JUDGMENT WHEN MAKING DECISIONS.

I HAVE PERFECT VISION AND CAN SEE THINGS CLEARLY.

I AM BALANCED PHYSICALLY, MENTALLY, AND SPIRITUALLY.

I SHARE MY CONCEPTS IN A LOVING, HELPFUL WAY.

I RESPECT OTHERS' OPINIONS.

MY EMOTIONS ARE ALWAYS UNDER CONTROL.

I RELEASE ANY OLD, LIMITING HABITS AND REPLACE THEM
WITH NEW, UPLIFTING ONES.

These are some ideas you may want to concentrate on to get
started. Negative thinking can sap your energy and creativity and
prevent you from realizing your goal.

You will find that it is fun being creative, and very quickly, it can
become a way of life for you. Become a positive, happy person. You
will have more friends and be more content.

UPLIFTING SAYINGS

Clip out every uplifting, humorous, or phrase that resonates with you as you read newspapers or magazines. Type them on a piece of paper and cut the paper to measure one inch wide by three inches long. Cut a plastic straw into 1/2 inch pieces. Roll the typed-out, uplifting, humorous sayings around a toothpick and insert it into the 1/2 inch straw. Place the sayings in a box or bowl and select several a day to read or meditate on. After reading, place them back into the container and keep adding to your collection. Soon you will be able to memorize them. I make boxes of uplifting sayings as personal gifts for my friends. Paste this message on the inside cover:

If it's an answer you wish to find,
Let it come from your subconscious mind,
Your hand will select the answer or clue,
To accept or reject is up to you!

Guests and friends enjoy selecting and reading uplifting or humorous messages. I place my rolled messages in a crystal compote bowl, twelve inches high. It sits on my coffee table.

Here is an example of a tiny saying Helene gave me. It measures 3" x 1".

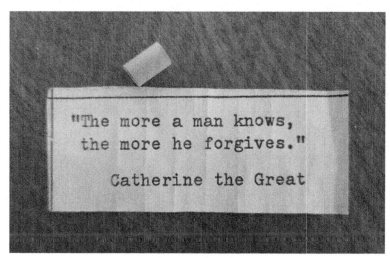

Here are some samples to give you an idea of the messages I clip:

"Humor is a hole that lets the sawdust out of a stuffed shirt."
—Jan McKeithen

It's hard to soar with eagles when you work with turkeys.

Are you aware that when you reach the bottom the next step is always UP?

Please be Patient...
God isn't with you yet!

TO MEDITATE,
do nothing more.

The PAST is dead,
the FUTURE is God's,
The PRESENT is ours!

'Who lives content with little, possesses everything."
—Despreaux

A man doesn't live by bread alone: he needs buttering up once in a while.

Its easier to suffer in silence if you are sure someone is watching

Ask and You Shall Receive

Luck is like a rubber crutch: It will let you down when you try to lean on it.

"FRIENDSHIP is like a treasury: you cannot take from it more than you put into it." —Mandelstamm

"Anybody who isn't pulling his weight is probably pushing luck.' —Franklin P. Jones

Today...I will listen, learn and UNDERSTAND all things I come in contact with.

OPEN your heart and share all things with the LORD, and you will never walk alone.

It is better to wear out than rust out.

'Life is beautiful when one sees beyond it.' —Bonnat

The very first step toward success in any job is to become interested in it.

When we do more, and ask for less—our lives are often more, fully blessed!

'It's hard to detect good luck— it looks so much like something you earned.' —Frank Clark

THE BEGINNING OF WISDOM IS SILENCE.

Even the EGOTIST is to be admired —he never goes around talking about others.

The truth may set you free, but it won't make you many friends.

"Never try to make anyone like you ,you know and God knows, that one of you is enough'
—Emerson

"Where love rules there is no will to power."
—Carl Jung

Argue for your limitations, and sure enough, they're yours.
—Richard Bach

We will find time for anything we care enough about.

A GIFT must be given with LOVE , or it is no gift at all.

How a man plays the game shows something of his character; how he loses shows all of it.

Open your mind
—the mind
is the doorway
to the SOUL.

"All that some people leave on the sands of time are seatprints."
—David Vincent

"Plastic surgery can do anything with the human nose except keep it out of other people's business."
—S. A. Norris

"All mankind is divided into three classes: those who are immovable; those who are movable;and those who move." —Benjamin Franklin

The BIGGEST step you can take is the one you take when you meet the other person halfway.

"The best way to get a friend, is to be one."
— Frank Clark

"The more a man knows, the more he forgives."
—Catherine the Great

When all else fails, lower your standards!

"PEACE is happiness digesting."
—Victor Hugo

Some people are like boats: they toot the loudest when they're in a fog.

BE DIFFERENT.
ACT NORMAL!

REINFORCING YOUR TALENTS & GREATNESS

Make a fifteen-minute tape. Include every constructive, positive suggestion you can think about. There are many excellent suggestions in self-help books. Listen to the tape before you go to sleep at night. Before getting out of bed in the morning, tell yourself: *"Today is the first day of the rest of my life, and it will be the greatest experience yet."* And it will be.

NOTE: You can use the recording device on your cell phone to create your own 'tape,' or there are many options on iTunes and YouTube you can listen to. Everything from binaural beats, Solfeggio frequencies to soothing meditations covering every topic you want to heal.

I read a most interesting article in one of the tape catalogs I received in the mail. It stated that the average person remembers only 75% of any information they hear after 24 hours. After 48 hours, they only remember 50%. After four days, they can recall only 15%, and after 16 days, they will remember only 2% of the original information. The article pointed out that in order to recall 62% of any information after several months, a person must hear something repeated six times or more.

For this reason, I suggest listening to the tape nightly for at least a month. This will almost guarantee you that not only will your thinking change, but your attitude will also. Remember—YOU ARE WHAT YOU THINK. I'm aware I shared Frank Outlaw's profound statement in an earlier part of this book, but it's worth repeating at this time.

Watch your thoughts, they become words;
watch your words, they become actions;
watch your actions, they become habits;
watch your habits, they become character;
watch your character, for it becomes your destiny.

How To Get Out Of A Rut

Relax in a comfortable position. Breathe deeply and mentally repeat: "With each breath, I am cleansing myself of worry, pain, envy, hate (or whatever you want to eliminate)."

This should only take about five minutes of your time. There are so many little things one can do to keep yourself happy and keep an uplifting outlook on life. By all means, walk the malls, the park, visit a friend, or exercise. Share only happy situations with friends. Avoid dwelling on your problems, for they are only 'projects' that you can solve. A wise man once said: "Don't tell people your problems. Fifty percent could care less, and the other fifty percent are glad you got 'em." Give that some thought.

Drawing Money To You

Buy a package of play money from the toy or game department of a store. Write your name on all the bills. Paste them on a piece of green cardboard. With a marks-a-lot, print: MY GOOD IS AT HAND, AND I AM GRATEFULLY RECEIVING IT NOW. MONEY IS DRAWN TO ME CONSTANTLY. MY MONEY SUPPLY IS LIMITLESS. Read it several times each day, and imagine you have a handful of money.

How About Lotteries?

That's a question I am asked quite frequently. I don't know. I have never had an opportunity to do research. Texas now has a state lottery. I do have some thoughts about how I would approach that sweepstakes. I would choose the numbers that had personal significance for me: my birth date, house number, or social security number. I would stay with the same numbers and keep giving energy to them by seeing myself being presented with a hefty amount on a check. It would be difficult to specify a certain amount because I understand the jackpot varies. Each state has different systems; some use six numbers, and some use eight. If your state lottery numbers are selected on TV, you certainly have an excellent opportunity to play the mind over matter game and mentally see your numbers being selected. The more positive one becomes, the faster the end results are realized.

CONTESTING FOR KIDS

As for contesting or entering sweepstakes, I now get great pleasure encouraging my grandson in these areas. He is showing an interest in the hobby. When my grandson was eight years old, he spent some of his summer vacation with me. I kept him busy being creative. The coloring contests he submitted paid off for him. In all, he entered five contests. He won three: $100 for a national magazine for drawing and coloring a picture of his family—second prize in another for coloring a pirate. The prize was a videocassette recorder with twelve videos. And a cereal box contest awarded him $100.

COLORING CONTESTS

In a coloring contest, you simply use crayons and color the picture. You read the rules carefully. Rules usually list how the picture will be judged. For example, creative use of coloring materials, 30%; overall artistic effect, 30%; interpretation of elements in the picture, 20%; neatness, 20%.

Let's explain. With all the crayon colors available and different shades of the same color, you have an opportunity to make pictures more creative with light and dark blends. Be more creative and embellish with interesting effects. A picture may have a beach scene: Why not color the sand tan, put a thin coat of glue over it, and sprinkle that part of the picture with real sand! To present a '3-D' effect entry: cut out the main character and paste it on a piece of cardboard; paste the back scene in a box the size of the picture. (Boxes can be purchased at any variety store in the gift wrap department.) You may want to glue in plastic greenery of small sizes to give it depth. Visit the craft department of any variety store for many more ideas. You may want to use round googly eyes that move. If people are in the picture that you are to color, you might want to dress them with dress material or blue jean material. How about using yarn for the hair?

Some materials have a shaggy texture that could be used on animals. If a water scene is in the picture, color it shades of blue. It gives the water a real wet look. Yes, there is a place for glitter, too. But children tend to go overboard. For Christmas and Winter scenes, it is okay in moderation.

How about a night scene to be different? If so, use deep blue for the sky and spangles for stars. Bear in mind that children's coloring contests are very popular, and the judges receive thousands of entries. After a while, they all start to look alike to the judges, so yours must be *different.*

For young children in the five-to-seven age bracket, let them look in coloring books to get ideas. If it calls for a drawing, they can get some ideas from them. Using an example is better than giving them a blank sheet of paper.

What did my grandson submit to win the $100 for the contest that required children to draw a picture of their family? After encouraging him to page through a story and coloring books, he decided on the illustration below. This is a copy of what he submitted. I made a copy from the original and added it to his GROWING UP scrapbook.

He used graph paper and a ruler to keep the picture neat. He pictured himself in his little league shirt and cap. When it came to drawing Mom, "She is always on the phone," he commented. It took several days to complete the drawing and coloring, with plenty of encouragement. When it was finished and mailed, I had to remind him that it would take several months before he might hear from the judges. I also reminded him to see himself opening the envelope and getting a check. Prizes in this contest were money. It took almost three months after the closing date before he received his $100 prize.

Judging firms will send out a winner's list if you request it. Some people like to know who won. If this interests you, you must send a self-addressed, stamped envelope and be sure to read the rules—the address to receive a winner's list is different from the address where you submit the coloring entry.

The other contest my grandson entered required him to color a picture of a pirate. The pirate was sitting on a beach. He did use real sand for the beach, and after coloring the water blue, he brushed on an overcoat of clear nail polish. He enjoys writing stories, so he wanted to make his entry like a storybook.

He used a folder and printed the title of the story on the cover: 'PETE THE KINDHEARTED PIRATE.' He really was excited about this project because the big prize was a family trip and a chest full of toys.

He received an affidavit on the first of December. In January, he received a letter telling him he won second prize, a videocassette recorder with twelve videos. In February, the prize was delivered.

Many times, a package will arrive with just a note saying you won the prize. It can be very exciting for children if they make coloring and drawing contests their hobby.

This year, our grandson was declared the most artistic student in his class of thirty. His painting of birds was displayed at the Civic Art Center. For that, he received a gold ribbon and his picture in the paper. Prior to entering coloring contests, he was not that interested in being creative. Encourage children while they are young. It not only can be profitable, but it develops talent in the artistic areas.

PART FOUR

BONUS MATERIAL

In 2003, Helene discovered that some people were selling her out-of-print books for $100 or more. She found this unacceptable and decided to print copies of *The Name It & Claim It Game* herself because her goal was to keep the sale price affordable so everyone could enjoy her wisdom. If you ordered a book from her, it was copied, cerloxed, perhaps even autographed, and mailed to you directly.

As I stated in the *Foreword*, Helene never stopped learning, growing, and, more importantly, teaching. She wasn't tech savvy, plus the technology at the time wasn't as robust as it is now, so she tacked any new material she wrote to the end of the book or the end of a chapter. Helene also emailed me several articles to share with my blog followers.

When creating this edition, I combined all those teachings into this *Bonus Material* section. This change allows you to enjoy all of Helene's stories, adventures, and lessons cohesively without losing the flow of her initial work because I know she would want to continue to learn and grow, just as she had.

HELENE'S PATH

This chapter was originally written as an *Afterword* for the 2003 edition Helene created at home. It was simply titled UPDATE.

UPDATE

Recently I had a question asked that I feel needs to be addressed. WHO ARE YOU? This is the way I answered it: AM I A CHOSEN ONE? I DON'T THINK SO. Saving the world is not my assignment. Unlike Sylvia Browne, the dead and I do not converse. Jeane Dixon made predictions; I do not.

I am told that I am simply a channel to help people help themselves. That is my mission this lifetime. I am given assignments by Beings from other dimensions that appear to me in a physical form and communicate telepathically. Rarely do the same Beings (entities) appear for each person—this leads me to believe that they are the individual's personal guide or guardian angel.

My assignments do not occur on a daily basis. In fact, they happen so sporadically, I still get startled when a Being does appear. But I am no longer frightened. When their visits first began, I would yell out, "Go away! Leave me alone! I must be going crazy." It was a number of years before I realized why they were coming. Yes, I received messages and explanations in dreams and in the meditative state, but I was reluctant to acknowledge their presence. It took a lot of patience and convincing on their part before I finally felt safe and confident enough to pursue an assignment.

Today, when a fourth-dimensional Being appears, I listen to their request, and I wait for three signs (my way of confirmation). I am never foolhardy enough to blurt out something that may only confuse people. In my book, *Confessions of an 83-Year-Old Sage,* I cite a number of examples where I requested proof before venturing into foreign territories.

There are many ways of helping and healing people in the physical, emotional, and spiritual realms. I realize that a doctor practicing traditional medicine is necessary when someone develops a chemistry imbalance or their skills are required when repairing a body after an accident.

Psychologists and counselors also serve a purpose by listening and offering suggestions when a person is going through mental trauma. Ministers, rabbis, and priests are available when one has doubts and questions about spiritual matters.

I heal with WORDS. The knowledge I convey does not come from books or from a college education; I simply repeat what is given to me telepathically by another dimensional Being who is present in the current meeting.

If a person is surprised by the solutions I suggest, I simply explain that this is one of those days that I'm good at guessing. There is no need to describe the Being (entity) that usually accompanies him or her when we meet; however, not all people have a Being accompanying them. When this occurs, I engage them in small talk about things such as family, current events, etc.

At age 79, I am enjoying my freedom and space and love being alone on my five acres in rural Alvarado, Texas. If I have the need for social contact, I let it be known that I am available. It's a technique I've used for the past 35 years. I repeat to my guardian, "Let me be a channel to help people to help themselves." It doesn't take long before the phone rings or a letter arrives with a request from a person who is looking for a place to regroup and relax or to simply come to my center to talk over life's little daily challenges we all encounter. They call them problems; I call them projects and learning experiences.

I feel fortunate that I am aware of other dimensions. Our three-dimensional world is our physical classroom for learning life's lessons. The fourth and other dimensions, the unseen worlds, are the homes of our counselors and guardians, those Beings who offer us guidance and assistance.

There are a number of people in today's society that operate in other dimensions as I do. I do feel blessed when we make contact with each other. The CHOSEN ONES? I don't think so. We know that we agreed to the role that we are playing before we came into a physical body and that our guardians are always nearby to help us and others who need encouragement and answers.

ADDITIONAL THOUGHT

I seldom watch TV. However, there are a few shows that caught my interest over the years.

I found the TV program **Joan of Arcadia** refreshing. Two newer shows I enjoy are **The Medium** and **Ghost Whisperer**.

Were the writers inspired to remind us that we are all surrounded by guardians that appear in many guises to help us during our lifetime? I believe this is why the stories were written, as many viewers are able to identify with Joan, Allison, and Melinda.

PHYSICIAN HEAL THYSELF

I discovered this chapter at the end of Helene's 2003 self-published, self-printed edition of *The Name It & Claim It Game*. It doesn't fit with her stories of positive thinking, manifesting, or the Law of Attraction, but as it wasn't included in any of her other books, I chose to share it. It may have been the inspiration for *Confessions of an 83-Year-Old Sage,* which she published in 2007, as all those stories are similar in nature.

The Visitor

The accident wasn't the only time I used the techniques I learned from José Silva.

"Hey, I've done that." I thought to myself as I was reading Rebecca Lattimer's book titled: *You're Not Old Until You're Ninety*. In chapter six of her book, she talks about an imaginary doctor she seeks advice from when she is physically or mentally having challenges. She said she read about it in a book titled: *The Well Body Book* by Mike Samuels. I was not familiar with that book, but I did take THE SILVA METHOD OF MENTAL TRAINING in the early seventies. One of the techniques we were taught was going to the Alpha level via relaxation and meeting with counselors to help us solve problems. I find that technique extremely beneficial, and today it is second nature for me to use it when I need an answer. Sometimes I see or feel a presence. Other times an answer just comes to me from out of the cosmos.

I keep a notebook and pen by my bedside and in the car to write down a keyword or phrase so that I can explore it at a more convenient time. That's what happened today while I was driving. The thought came to write my experience about the doctor that appeared to me while I was going through a big-time physical challenge. The title of the story should be Physician Heal Thyself. Perhaps the idea came to mind because I was reading. *You're Not Old Until You're Ninety* earlier that morning.

It was early July 1992, after sixty-six years of being in this body, when the discomfort in my abdomen became a nuisance. I tried to ignore it because I lost confidence in the medical profession due to a number of unpleasant experiences in the past. But I knew I could no longer ignore it. I sensed there was something seriously wrong with my elimination process, and it needed attention.

Earlier that year, I was invited to be the key speaker at the Silva Mental Training convention in Laredo on August 11th. I decided to postpone going to the doctor until after the convention because I was looking forward to touching base with the many friends I met while working with José Silva, founder of the program.

One morning after an uncomfortable night, I was in my recliner sipping tea when I had a visitor from the 'Twilight Zone.' (The Twilight Zone, for me, is the fourth dimension where a number of people, including myself, can see and communicate with spirit beings.) I firmly believe that some of the visitors we see are thought forms we create and some apparitions that come to guide us in our time of need. (My book *In Contact With Other Realms* explains thought forms and apparitions in more detail.)

The visitor who appeared was small in stature and looked to be about sixty years of age. His deep-lined forehead and slanted eyes told me he must be Asian. He wore a loose white knee-length coat over white slacks, which led me to believe he was a doctor. It was his eyes that fascinated me. They were like summer lightning one minute, the next a clear soft blue. I sensed wisdom, intelligence, and understanding behind those eyes.

"Your body needs attention on the physical plane. You have been neglecting it for too long, and it's time to take care of it now," he communicated as he stood in front of me. I felt confident that he was there to help me, so I took his advice.

That afternoon I made an appointment to see a physical doctor. After an examination and hearing my symptoms, the doctor recommended an internal scan and x-rays. "Let's get this over with as soon as possible," I requested.

The following morning I took a battery of tests as an outpatient. Two days later, I was back in the doctor's office to hear the results.

The doctor had the x-rays displayed on the wall when I arrived. He pointed to a mass on my bladder that was causing the problem and recommended that immediate surgery was necessary.

"I will not be able to do the surgery because it looks like cancer. I feel an oncologist should do the surgery, and I can recommend several top surgeons in Dallas. I can make an appointment today," he offered.

"But I can't have cancer. I never learned to develop it," I said as my heart thumped uncomfortably. He stared at me for a second, probably baffled at my response, and explained, "I've consulted with two of my colleagues. They agree surgery is required." Before I left the office, his nurse made an appointment for me to see the oncologist.

That night as I lay in bed reviewing what I was about to face, the doctor from the Twilight Zone reappeared. "No. There is no cancer. It is an infection around a tumor that is blocking your organs. It must be removed. You will be fine, and I recommend that you approach this experience with humor."

"You gotta be kidding," I said out loud when I heard that suggestion.

"No. I am not joking. It is a much better approach than fear, and I will be by your side to help you through this learning experience," he assured me.

Two days later, I was in the waiting room of the oncologist. After we met, he immediately led me to his examination room, where my x-rays were displayed. He had circled the tumor and said it definitely needed to be removed.

"Can you tell… is it a boy or a girl?" I questioned with a serious tone.

"Mrs. Hadsell, I understand you are over sixty years of age, and it's unlikely you could be pregnant," he patiently explained.

I kept up the serious tone and said, "I guess you don't read the National Enquirer. Space aliens have been coming down and impregnating women for quite some time now." After a moment of silence, he picked up my medical file, looked at it briefly, then asked, "Mrs. Hadsell, have you had a brain scan?"

"Why no, why would you ask that?"

"Because what you are about to undertake is serious," he said as his face clouded with concern.

"OK. Let's make a deal. You be serious, and I'll be silly. Lighten up. It's joke time," I said, trying to put him at ease. He was only casually amused as he ushered me into his office so we could discuss the next steps that would be taken.

"I'll make all the arrangements, and we can schedule the surgery for next Friday," he said after looking at the appointment calendar on his desk. "You need to fill out a consent form to have blood transfusions," he explained, handing me the paper for me to sign.

"Why is that necessary?" I asked.

"It's a precautionary measure. I have found patients in your age group bleed more during major surgery, and I just want to be prepared," he explained.

"I'm glad you called that to my attention. I will stop the bleeding, so that should be no problem for you."

"You will what?!" he muttered as he gave me an 'I can't believe what I just heard' look.

I sensed that last remark needed an explanation, so I began. "It's a mind-over-matter technique I've used in the past. It's quite effective. That's one less complication you have to be concerned about," I assured him.

"I want to have the surgery Monday morning," I added as I felt this doctor would be the one that could help heal this body.

"That's impossible. I'll need to reserve the operating room and contact an anesthetist and another doctor to prepare," he explained.

"Well then, don't just sit there. Get on the phone and make it happen. I want to get this over with as soon as possible, so I can get on with life."

Too startled by my request to offer any objection, he got on the phone, and within fifteen minutes, all the arrangements were made.

I was to spend the night in a hotel annex in the hospital, so I could report Monday morning at 7:00 AM for the surgery. Yes. I was scared. I would be lying if I said I wasn't, but for some strange reason, I KNEW it was the thing to do, and I would be OK.

After arriving home that afternoon, I headed for my recliner to review the day's activities. My Twilight Zone doctor was sitting in a chair in front of me, ready to help me sort things out.

"Now, let's review what is in store for you. You will have sufficiently recovered to speak at the convention. There will be some discomfort, which you must accept, as that is just an unpleasant experience one has to bear while in a physical body. You will be able to handle it sufficiently with the techniques you witnessed during your stay in Russia. Remember, everything is energy. Healing energy comes in

pulsations. When you give it negative energy with fear, it can become almost unbearable. When you repeat—healing... healing... healing instead of hurting... hurting... hurting—the energy changes and feels like waves of soothing soft strokes, and the body heals more rapidly. Review all this information so you can prepare yourself," he suggested.

I have what some people may consider a hang-up. I chose not to tell or discuss my physical problems with family or friends because I know how the mind works. Just the word cancer frightens people. The first thing they think about is how many people they know that have had cancer and how they suffered. The next thing they do, they think of me, and I pick up on their thoughts and fears and have to deal with not only my thoughts but theirs. So, the only person that knew I was going in for surgery was my husband Pat because he also knows how the mind works. I could count on him for support. I didn't even tell my children. That was my choice at the time. I didn't need their sympathy. They couldn't do anything except worry. I knew if they were needed, they would be the first there to help me.

Monday morning, after checking into the hospital, I was put in a small room with a nurse. I put on a gown and was given a shot. Five hours later, I opened my eyes and saw two doctors, the anesthetist, and my husband standing around my bed. The doctor was anxious to ask questions.

"We want to know how you stopped the bleeding," the anesthetist asked.

"She talks to her body and tells it how to behave," my husband answered, relieved I would be alright. I was immediately aware of all the tubes attached to my body. My goal was to get out of that place as soon as possible.

"When you feel pain, just press this button and self-medicate yourself with drugs," the doctor showed me. I never pressed the button. When I was aware of discomfort, I mentally changed the pain pulsations to healing waves of energy.

The following morning when the doctor came by to check in on me, he shook the plastic drug bag and asked the nurse if they hooked up another bag. She replied they hadn't.

"Don't you have any pain?" the doctor asked with concern.

"Yes, I do, but I want to clear out my system of drugs so the body can heal on its own. I don't want to depend on drugs," I explained.

"You are probably one of those people that has a high threshold for pain," he rationalized.

No, I didn't tell him that my doctor from the Twilight Zone was giving better advice than he was. I was out of the hospital in three days and presented my speech at the convention two weeks later.

Funny thing, the doctor from the Twilight Zone only appears when I need advice about a physical, mental, or emotional challenge.

By the way, did I mention what he said when I asked what his name is?

"Physician Heal Thyself," he replied as his gentle laugh rippled through the air.

"If it pleases, you may refer to me as DOCTOR I KNOW!"

MY SILVA LININGS

I was paging through one of the many journals that I kept after I took the Silva Mind Development classes in the early 70s. I came across so many interesting personal experiences that I would like to share some of them with you. The following is one. I'm sure some of the incidents you can relate to, and some you may want to research on your own.

We formed groups and met weekly to review what we were taught. Our main interests were in the healing arts... detecting abnormalities on our mental screen and concentrating healing energy to those areas. The students reported their successes and were elated. But many times, the projection of sending energy for any purpose was not lasting; that is when I learned that when one sends energy for any purpose, the energy dissipates after 72 hours. (I learned this while in Russia after I met with some of the healers from all over the world that were in attendance.) After I became aware of this information, it was suggested we should send energy for a person's highest good, as who are we to know what they have to learn or experience this lifetime? And this is what I have been doing ever since.

One Tuesday afternoon, I received a phone call from a woman requesting that we send healing energy to her brother. He was only 32-years-old and in the hospital with stomach cancer.

She told me that her church members met nightly praying for his healing and that he did show signs of improvement. She felt that if we included him in our energy circle, he would be healed. After taking his name to include him at that night's meeting and getting her phone number, I informed her that I would like to keep in touch.

That evening when the students projected him on their mental screen, we all learned something. They were given his first name and age, and they were to sense what his problem was. We then would discuss what we picked up about him. He telepathically let us know that he did not want any more energy or prayers and that we were holding him back from leaving his body. When we asked why he wanted to die at such a young age, he replied, "My time in the physical is done. I came to teach responsibility to my family, and it has been accomplished. Now leave me alone."

The next morning I intended to call his sister and tell her what we learned, but she contacted me first. "Mrs. Hadsell, I had a most disturbing dream last night. My brother appeared in a dream and told me to please stop praying for his healing because the energy was holding him back from leaving his body. So please take him off of your healing list," she requested.

Since that time, I will only project energy for a person's highest good. And now you, too, are aware that when we project energy, it lasts 72 hours. At this stage of my life, I have no more needs but still have a few wants. When I project energy for a want, I stipulate that it materialize only if it is for my highest good.

BLUEPRINTS #1

As I describe in the *My Adventures With Helene* chapter, the Blueprints were made in photo albums with sticky pages. Upon those pages, Helene compiled information from various modalities (see below) based on your birthdate to give you a glimpse into your soul's journey.

Until recently, I didn't know of anyone offering the type of Blueprints Helene created. It is why I included her articles in this book, with the hope that you will glean insight into your own path.

Then psychic medium, Sarah Jordon, following her intuition, contacted me about recreating, as closely as possible, Helene's Blueprints. Blueprints 2.0 are now available here: https://bit.ly/Blueprints2

NOTE: You can watch two videos about Helene's Blueprints on my WordsForWinning YouTube channel. https://www.youtube.com/@WordsForWinning

If you would like additional help in discovering your destiny, there are countless good readers, intuitives, psychics, and mediums that specialize in astrology, numerology, oracles, energy work, feng shui, etc. Begin with the *Recommended Reading* resources I outline at the end of this book and go from there.

The following formula that I have used for the past 50 years to compile Blueprints is called UNITOLOGY. It includes Astrology, Numerology, Playing Cards, Chinese Astrology, KI-ology, Karmic Ties, Master Numbers, Past Life techniques, Toning (which is your personal note to resonate healing), your Personal Year charted, plus a review and suggestions and impressions that I am led to share with the person.

NOTE: The way Helene uses the word UNITOLOGY means; the unity of all types of metaphysical and spiritual methodologies to discover your life path, purpose, and flow with divine timing, versus a religious church or cult using the same term.

UNITOLOGY is neither a religion nor a form of fortune-telling; rather, it is a method for timing your decisions and actions with the rhythm of life. KNOW that you can change your destiny when you change your thinking. UNITOLOGY can fulfill the need of people that are eagerly searching for a person or book that can help them in human understanding. The simplicity of this method of self-analysis is the answer that I still use today.

I present the personalized information in a twenty-page photo album so that one can refer to it periodically. The following is an explanation I share from my personal experiences and research. You may accept or reject my opinions.

You chose your parents. Your parents gave you a name. Your higher self gave you your MISSION. As you read and review your Blueprint, always Accentuate the positive and Eliminate the negative.

Our life is divided into three major cycles. The first major cycle is the MONTH number. This cycle represents the FORMATIVE years and sets the tone for the entire life. It also represents the condition in which you were born. This is the cycle when you form your value and belief systems. It represents experiences related to your family, childhood, schooling, religion, and your environment. PYTHAGORAS taught that there are NINE BASIC NUMBERS; all else is REPETITION. Therefore, whenever we encounter a compound number, we reduce it to a single digit. Unless it adds up to an 11, 22, or 33, which we call MASTER NUMBERS, this means that you have more energy to work with.

Each lifetime that we are on planet earth in a physical body, we have a MISSION, also referred to as our DESTINY NUMBER. How we find that number is by adding your birth date numbers and reduce them until you get a single digit. For example, if your birthday is September 4, 1960 (9/4/1960), you obtain your Mission/Destiny Number like this: 9+4+1960 = 1973. 1+9+7+3=20. 2+0=2. Your Mission/Destiny Number is 2.

NOTE: You could also add the date like this: 9+4+1+9+6+0 = 29 then 2+9=11 and finally 1+1=2.

I used to be amazed how many people had no idea what their Mission/Destiny is. People from all walks of life and from all over the world are now requesting to have their Blueprint charted.

BLUEPRINTS #2

After Helene was featured in a 2008 Finerminds (now Mindvalley) educational program (no longer available), she was flooded with inquiries about her books, Blueprints, and specifically her SPEC method from people worldwide. Many were worried about their current economic situation or wanted to know why they weren't winning money. She asked me to share this with my readers.

EXPLAINING A BLUEPRINT

I enjoy doing people's Blueprints. It offers so much information about the MISSION one comes into a physical body to experience this lifetime. I have had so many requests to explain how I set up a chart that I decided to explain and give you a clearer picture of what it is all about.

EXAMPLE: A male born September 7, 1960. (We only work with numbers from 1 to 9, so I add the year to get a 7.) September is a (9). Day is a (7). Year is 1960 = (7). Add the 9+7+7 = 23. 2+3 = (5). His Mission is the ADVENTURER—one who grows and learns about life through being willing to live it to the hilt and to change things (and people). It represents freedom.

Each Blueprint includes what your name means, your Informative, Productive, and Harvest cycles. I request three birth dates of family or friends that you wish to learn more about, so I can show you the karmic ties you have with them. I also include the technique of how you can chart information about other people's Mission. One of the most revealing aspects of each Blueprint is the playing card chosen according to your birth. I also include a card for each person that you included. Your Sun Sign, where your North Node was at your birth, informing you about what you need to work on while in your physical body; the Tone that resonates with your Sun Sign. Master numbers are revealed in birth numbers. Your Chinese animal, KI-ology, and plenty of cartoons, so that you can lighten up while you read all the information about you.

The part that I personally enjoy the most about doing a Blueprint is when I complete it, sit back to read it, and write information that you need to consider. Many times I feel that someone is mentally communicating to me what I should remind you of. When this happens, I feel I learn as much or more than the person whose Blueprint I am doing. Let me share an actual page that I wrote to the man whose chart I did a number of months ago. You recall he was born September 7, 1960.

SOMETHINGS FOR YOU TO CONSIDER

You have some interesting numbers to work within this incarnation—remember that your parents gave you your name—higher intelligence gave you your numbers.

September a (9) month is your INFORMATION cycle that lasts until you are 31 years old. The (9) is the vibration of the Humanitarian—whose life must be an example of the realization that all people and all life forms are interdependent. You must learn to cope, as it requires great amounts of understanding. During this period, you were serious and desperately trying to rationalize many things you couldn't understand because you had a restless streak that pulled you every which way. You did a lot of reading. Did you know that you have a natural talent to write—a gift that you had in past lives? I hope that you are aware of this writing talent. This was not an easy cycle for you. It urged you to pursue self-knowledge. It required a lot of soul-searching because your MISSION—as the Adventurer is restless—wants to travel/investigate. Writing your feelings and experiences would have been a great comfort. Perhaps a journal that you could have referred to occasionally would have been most beneficial. But you are no longer in this cycle.

Day born a (7) Your PRODUCTIVE cycle from age 32 to 58 and what you are presently in is the number of the Philosopher—whose inner journey ends only at complete self-knowledge and perfected lifestyle. To spend a lot of time analyzing would be a good habit to cultivate.

Your HARVEST cycle is also (7), and it begins when you are 59 years old. You have been dealt a double seven, the Productive and Harvest cycle. Are you getting the message that you need to focus on the spiritual aspect of who you are—why you are here and what you are here to learn? I note on your karmic tie page that YOU, your WIFE, and SON all have the number (7) in your Harvest cycle. You all came from the same Soul Group Soul to support each other. Your card—The Queen of Hearts-The Loving Mother Card—has excellent information and suggestions that can be most beneficial for you to consider. The Desiderata, on the back cover of your 20-page Blueprint book, has a down-to-earth philosophy that makes a lot of sense. You will be in your physical body for a long time. Be assured that you will LIVE, not just exist. Fun and games are still in store for you. Lighten up kid… that's why I included all the cartoons for your benefit. ENJOY!

The man whose Blueprint I just shared with you asked me this question, "Can you please explain in detail how to project prosperity?"

MY ANSWER

I can't be more specific than what I have repeated thousands of times SPEC! **S**elect It… **P**roject It… **E**xpect It… **C**ollect It…

See yourself as already having what it is you want. Now that you are aware of what you came into this lifetime to accomplish, there will come a time that cars, trips, houses, money, prosperity will not be a priority. Therefore I suggest that you add this to your goals, wishes, and projects. *'If it's meant to be,'* or *'If this is for my highest good'.* José Silva used the phrase, *"God willing."* I personally believe that we are given everything that we earned in our past and present life. We must ask to receive—that's what SPEC is all about.

May I remind you that you contacted me to do your Blueprint and that you may accept or reject anything that I have said. I realize that I may lose friends and influence enemies, but that's what I get for being an old SAGE.

Fourteen Karats of Gold

As I previously stated, Helene never stopped learning or teaching. In her last year of life, she was inspired by the Olympic games and asked me to share the following article for you to enjoy.

Are You A Gold, Silver or Bronze Winner?
The 2010 Olympic awards medals for physical performances; I propose that we have awards for anyone that uses their mind, imagination and benevolent actions on a daily basis.

Answer the following questions to see how you rate.

1. Do you act on your emotions? Logic may provide the reason for buying or doing something, but emotion supplies the urge.

2. Are you using your sixth sense, a knowing that just happens? If so, you can move mountains with persistence and determination.

3. I once read people are divided into three groups: (1) those who make things happen, (2) those who watch things happen, and (3) those who wonder, *"What happened?"*. Do you make things happen?

4. I dislike the saying, *"Never cross a bridge until you come to it."* The world is owned by men and women who cross bridges in their imagination miles and miles in advance of the procession. Are you one of those people?

5. Do you try to make the most of all that comes and the least of all that goes?

6. What you think means more than anything else in your life, more than what you earn, more than where you live, more than your social position, and more than what anyone else may think about you. Are you aware of this?

7. Wholeheartedness is contagious. Give of yourself if you want to get it from others. Are you practicing this rule?

8. Have you always been able to tell when you're on the right track because that track has always been uphill?

9. Are you like a duck? Calm and unruffled on the surface, paddling like the devil underneath.

10. Have you learned that it's not who is right, but what is right that matters?

11. Are you aware that your goodwill is the only asset that competition cannot undersell or destroy?

12. Did you know that if you look successful, you're going to be successful? People will have confidence in you if you look like you have confidence in yourself.

13. Did you know that when you can do the common things in life in an uncommon way, you can command the attention of the world?

14. If you do what you feel when you feel it, you could continue to go beyond. It seems that when you're young, you worry about what everyone thinks about you. At about age 30, you may come to realize the world wasn't paying that close attention. Have you learned that yet?

Qualifications:

To qualify for a GOLD Medal, you must have had the perfect score of 14.

To qualify for a SILVER Medal, you must have answered yes to 10 questions.

To qualify for a BRONZE Medal, you must have scored 8 points.

Anyone that has fewer than 8 points needs an Attitude Adjustment.

DESIDERATA

GO PLACIDLY amid the noise and the haste, and remember what peace there may be in silence. As far as possible, without surrender, be on good terms with all persons.

Speak your truth quietly and clearly, and listen to others, even to the dull and the ignorant; they, too, have their story.

Avoid loud and aggressive persons; they are vexatious to the spirit. If you compare yourself with others, you may become vain or bitter, for always there will be greater and lesser persons than yourself.

Enjoy your achievements as well as your plans. Keep interested in your own career, however humble; it is a real possession in the changing fortunes of time.

Exercise caution in your business affairs, for the world is full of trickery. But let this not blind you to what virtue there is; many persons strive for high ideals, and everywhere life is full of heroism.

Be yourself. Especially do not feign affection. Neither be cynical about love, for in the face of all aridity and disenchantment, it is as perennial as the grass.

Take kindly the counsel of the years, gracefully surrendering the things of youth.

Nurture strength of spirit to shield you in sudden misfortune. But do not distress yourself with dark imaginings. Many fears are born of fatigue and loneliness.

Beyond a wholesome discipline, be gentle with yourself. You are a child of the universe no less than the trees and the stars; you have a right to be here.

And whether or not it is clear to you, no doubt the universe is unfolding as it should. Therefore, be at peace with God, whatever you conceive Him to be. And whatever your labors and aspirations, in the noisy confusion of life, keep peace in your soul. With all its sham, drudgery, and broken dreams, it is still a beautiful world. Be cheerful. Strive to be happy.

By Max Ehrmann © 1927

AFTERWORD

I had the good fortune to first read *The Name It & Claim It Game* over 15 years ago. I thought I fully understood Select It, Project It, Expect It, Collect It (SPEC) because I successfully manifested a trip to London, UK, using all of Helene's teachings.

Then, as I began to update this book and reading Helene's words over and over as I edited the wisdom she shared with the world so many years ago, I felt as if I was reading a whole new book. I understand her ideas and teachings differently. I believe it's because as we move through life, learn, grow, and evolve, so does the lens through which we view the world.

What I missed the first time around was right in the title. Helene was teaching all of us that it's a GAME. The key to SPEC is to HAVE FUN. Helene wrote this book about how to win prizes, but that was how she got you to read her ideas. This book is really about winning in life.

Do as Helene wanted you to do: play with it. SPEC anything and everything your heart desires. Don't worry if your dreams do not manifest immediately. Sometimes they're meant to take time. You must release the HOW; how it arrives or looks. (Remember Helene's trip to Paris? It was piecemealed together, but in the end, she was exactly where she wanted to be.) Enjoy the entire process from dreaming to receiving.

Don't wait over a decade to revisit Helene's teachings as I did. Make reading her wise words an annual event. Look at her lessons with fresh eyes every year, set new goals, and relish every adventure as you navigate the GAME of life.

If you give your wishes enough energy, they will manifest.
This is not wishful thinking; it's a fact.

Helene Hadsell

RECOMMENDED READING

Some of the books Helene mentions are now out of print but no less valuable. Be sure to scour used bookstores, thrift shops, and flea markets for old copies.

HELENE'S RECOMMENDATIONS

1. The Power of Positive Thinking
by Norman Vincent Peale

This is the book Helene mentions in Introduction #1 that set her on her winning path. The two points that enticed her to conduct further research on positivity and the mind were:

1. You can have anything you want as long as you know what it is.
2. See yourself as already having it.

2. The Silva Mind Control Method
by José Silva

Helene was not only friends with José Silva for over 30 years, but at one point, she was his Assistant and PR Manager. If you have any trouble mastering Select It, Project It, Expect It, Collect It (SPEC), a manifesting method Helene teaches in her first book, *The Name It & Claim It Game*, you must read José's book. Although Helene created SPEC years after she stopped working for Jose, you can see his influence and how SPEC dovetails into The Silva Method.

3. You're Not Old Until You're 90
by Rebecca Lattimer

Helene comments about reading this book in the Physician Heal Thyself chapter.

4. The Well Body Book
by Mike Samuels

Although Helene had never read this book, she did mention it. She did so to show the progression of passing knowledge forward. Each teacher leads you to the next. Each lesson learned can be updated and modernized for the next generation of students.

5. It Works: The Famous Little Red Book That Makes Your Dreams Come True!
by RHJ

Helene recommends this book in the WINeuvers For WISHcraft chapter as an augmentation to her lesson.

6. The Power of the Subconscious Mind
by Dr. Joseph Murphy

Helene was also friends with Dr. Joseph Murphy. As she states so often, it's good to repeat the same lessons several times to solidify them in our minds. It's also good to hear similar lessons from different teachers. Sometimes hearing the same concept presented from a slightly different angle helps us more fully grasp the idea.

CAROLYN'S RECOMMENDATIONS

1. The Law of Attraction
by Michael Losier

If you have trouble removing doubt from the equation as Helene instructs, then Michael's book is a must-read. His is the How-To Law of Attraction book, taking you through the process step-by-step, including how to manifest your desires by allowing.

2. The Attractor Factor
by Dr. Joe Vitale

Helene loved Joe. She thought he was very dynamic. The weekend I was with Helene, we reached out to Joe to see if we could hang out with him. Alas, it was not meant to be. If you read any of his books, you will understand why Helene liked him as a teacher.

3. Transforming Fate into Destiny
by Robert Ohotto

In life, like cards, the hand we are dealt is our Fate. How we play that hand is our Destiny. Robert teaches you how to identify and heal unconscious blocks that may be obstructing your highest good.

4. How To Win Cash, Cars, Trips & More!
by Carolyn Wilman

Helene and I had the same goal; teaching others how to enhance their lives by being positive, having fun, and winning prizes. If you want to learn step-by-step how to find, organize, enter, and win legitimate sweepstakes, contests, and giveaways, then my book is a must-read.

5. The Luck Factor
by Dr. Richard Wiseman

This is one of my favorite books because it shows you luck isn't some elusive mystical woodland creature never to be seen. Richard outlines four main principles that you can implement to create luck in your life.

6. The Spontaneous Fulfillment of Desire
by Deepak Chopra

There are no coincidences. For example, it wasn't a coincidence I learned about Helene and read her book(s) but also spent four days with her as well. It set up the opportunity for me to eventually share her work.

In his book, you will discover how we are all connected to everything that exists and everything that is yet to come. The more aware you become and connect to the field of infinite possibilities, the more 'coincidences' you experience.

7. Becoming Supernatural
by Dr. Joe Dispenza

As already stated, every teacher is a stepping stone to the next lesson and level of knowledge. Joe has learned from masters like José and is teaching the next level of mastering the mind. Through various meditations, you will learn how to tune into Universal energies and create the life you desire.

8. Heal Your Body
by Louise Hay

Similar to Helene, Louise healed herself. Her experience was so profound; not only did she write this book, along with many others,

Louise founded a publishing firm, Hay House. This book is a fantastic introduction to the mind-body-spirit connection.

9. **The Prize Winner of Defiance Ohio**
by Terry Ryan

The book is a must-read for anyone who loves to enter contests. (Be sure to read the book before you watch the movie.) The story chronicles the life of Evelyn Ryan and how she was able to use her Madison Avenue-style wit and creativity to raise her ten children in twenty-five words or less.

NOTE: If you want to read more of my favorites, you can find a more comprehensive list on my Words For Winning website: http://bit.ly/CarolynsFavoriteBooks

AUTHORS

HELENE HADSELL

Helene Hadsell's life was proof not only of her dynamic philosophy but also of her practice of positive thinking in the energetic pursuit of her goals, brought her rich rewards in terms of spiritual, physical, and material well-being. This book is her true account of the amazing events of her life that bear out her conviction that anyone can achieve anything their mind can conceive if they firmly resolve to do so.

Helene holds the unique record of having submitted the winning entry for every contest prize she ever wanted. She began contesting in 1957 and won everything from sports equipment to electric appliances, a Hammond organ, and trips to New York, Washington D.C., and Europe. Of course, Helene's biggest prize of all was winning a fully furnished dream home in a contest sponsored by the Formica Corporation.

In 1986 she founded Delta Sciences as a retreat center. People came from all over the world, including England, Switzerland, Hungary, and Peru, as well as from every state in the USA.

Helene Hadsell was the mother of three children: Pamela, Dike and Chris. She also had three grandchildren and three great-grandchildren. She lived in Alvarado, Texas, with her husband Pat, who shared her interest in helping people improve their lives through mental power.

CAROLYN WILMAN

Carolyn Wilman loves teaching others about Mindset, Marketing, and how to WIN! (both in life & sweepstakes.)

Under the banner of her agency, Idea Majesty—Carolyn specializes in Sweepstakes Marketing, helping companies and entrants connect.

Destined to help others live out their potential, Carolyn founded a publishing company—Words For Winning—that purchases publishing rights from out-of-print authors and thought leaders. She then updates and reintroduces their books to a new generation of readers.

To date, she has re-published all of Helene Hadsell's books. Helene was famous for winning every prize she ever desired, including a fully furnished home. Carolyn has also purchased the rights to many of Drs.Tag & Judith Powell's books. Interestingly, Tag was Helene's second publisher and an author in his own right.

Additionally, Carolyn is a Sweepstakes Teacher and is known as— The Contest Queen—she also wrote two award-winning books, *You Can't Win If You Don't Enter* and *How To Win Cash, Cars, Trips & More!* Her proven online entry system has helped others win more than $1M in cash and prizes.

As a contestor, similar to Helene, Carolyn herself has won over $350,000 in prizes over the past 20+ years, including trips to California, Florida, the Winter Olympics, a European tour, with a trip to the set of Harry Potter in London, England being her favorite.

Stay tuned to see what winning adventures will be next!

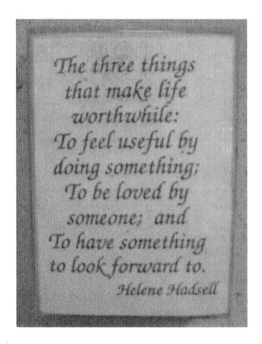

The three things
that make life
worthwhile:
To feel useful by
doing something;
To be loved by
someone; and
To have something
to look forward to.
Helene Hadsell